SOUTHERN NOR'

Showing principle destinations :
Motor Tanker Prowe

whilst Charlie Fielder was employed aboa

Knollendam
Wormerveer
Zaandijk
Koog aan de Zaan
Zaandam

Ijmuiden

Amsterdam

Vlardingen
● Zwijndrecht

● Bergen op Zoom

● Antwerp
(Kattendijk)

0   50   100
                              Nautical
                              Miles

THE
PROWESS
OF
CHARLIE
FIELDER

Compiled by
David G. Wood
with the assistance of other members of the
Society for Sailing Barge Research

Editing and further research by
Richard Walsh

CHAFFCUTTER

**Pre-press, production and publication by Chaffcutter Books
on behalf of the Society for Sailing Barge Research, 2014**

www.chaffcutter.com
www.sailingbargeresearch.org.uk

ISBN 978-0-9560596-2-8

*Images are credited to their source and copyright holder in the Picture Source
index. Although the origin, provenance and ultimate source of some images
remains obscure, every effort has been made to identify copyright holders and
obtain appropriate permissions for their inclusion in this publication.*

***Some photographs are from poor quality originals, but are included here
because of their historical relevance. Picture sources are listed at the back
of this book.***

Society for Sailing Barge Research,
Secretary - John White
5, Cox Road, Alresford, Colchester, Essex, CO7 8EJ

Published by
Chaffcutter Books,
39 Friars Road, Braughing, Ware, Hertfordshire SG11 2NN

Printed and bound in Great Britain by
Berforts Information Press,
23/25 Gunnels Wood Park, Gunnels Wood Road, Stevenage, Hertfordshire, SG1 2BH

The Society for Sailing Barge Research

Over 50 years ago, a group of enthusiasts recognised the importance of recording the fast diminishing number of sailing cargo vessels operating in the coastal and estuarial trades of our island nation. They logged the hulks, laid-up craft and the active fleet of the Thames sailing barge genre, and founded the Society for Spritsail Barge Research. Since that time the Society, now renamed the Society for Sailing Barge Research, to reflect a broadening interest in other cargo carrying sailing vessels around the coastline, has continued to investigate the history of the barges themselves, the way of life of those who crewed in them, the cargoes carried and the ports they served. In the years since its founding, the Society and its members have so far published around a million words and five thousand photographs on the subject.

Cargo carrying under sail finished in 1970, and whilst a small number of the Sailormen, as the craft and their crews were collectively known, continued under power for a few more years, now just a handful survive in active commission, charter parties and business guests replacing the grain, coal and cement cargoes of yesteryear. Though recognised as an important part of our maritime heritage, today's costs of preservation and restoration appear beyond the scope of many owners; craft that were active in the recent past, now destined to be hulked or broken up, the modest current fleet continuing to dwindle towards potential extinction.

The Society's fortunes, however, seem more stable, with membership double that of twenty years ago. For just £20 per annum, retired and present day bargemen, amateur sailormen, academics, students, artists, model-makers, those with family connections, enthusiasts of every hue, enjoy getting the twice-yearly magazine Mainsheet, and Topsail, the annual historical publication of the Society. Members are also able to make use of the Society's ever-growing Archive, where more than 15,000 photographs and documents are preserved to satisfy the interests of the membership and future generations.

Join us and enjoy the heritage of the sailing barge. An application form appears at the end of this book.

To Glynis, who realised
the significance of her uncle's suitcase,
the Twickenham Museum who secured it,
and the Members of
The Society for Sailing Barge Research,
who together expanded the background of this story.

This book reflects the time 'at sea' of Charlie Fielder, both under sail, steam and motor, embracing the annotated writings of the Master and Mate of a coastal tanker as recorded in her deck logbook and other papers in the Fielder Archive, with observations from public records.

Throughout this book, all illustrations are of the period of the narrative, unless otherwise noted within the caption.

CONTENTS

ACKNOWLEDGEMENTS

In addition to Charlie himself, we are indebted to Mrs. Feichtlbauer for her reminiscences of her uncle and help in tracing something of the Fielder family history; to Ann Wheldon, the Archivist of the London Borough of Hammersmith; to Jean Lear and Alison Cable at Medway Archives and Local Studies Centre; to Martin Salmon at the National Maritime Museum and to Dr. Mary Mills of the Greater London Industrial Archaeology Society.

A big thank-you to Patricia O' Driscoll, a former editor of Bygone Kent and Coast & Country Magazine; to Rob Cottrell and the Company of Watermen and Lightermen of the River Thames and to Sarah Williams, Claire Frankland and colleagues at the Museum in Docklands, who made available images and the records of the Port of London Authority and its predecessors.

We are indebted to Lyn Crawford at the Mitchell Library, Glasgow; also north of the border, the helpful team at Fife County Libraries & Museums. At the opposite end of the nation thanks also to Lois Woods at Poole Museum; Andrew Burt at Thurrock Museum; Johanna O'Donohue at Gt. Yarmouth's excellent Time & Tide Museum; Caroline Rhodes at Hull Museums; Barry Attoe and Sally Jennings at the British Postal Museum & Archive; the staff of the Royal Navy Museum; the Newham Council archives and to Vaughan Roberts at English Heritage.

In particular we must thank Ken Garrett for allowing use of the data and images from his book 'Everard of Greenhithe', published by the World Ship Society in 1991 (ISBN 0-9056175-8-4). An updated edition of 'Everard of Greenhithe' is in preparation.

Thanks go Peter Payan of the Twickenham Museum for steering the Fielder Archive to the Society for Sailing Barge Research enabling the preparation of this book; to Wendy Hawke at London Metropolitan Archives and to Julie Cochrane and Mike Bevan of the Royal Museums Greenwich, for access to the Fielder material after it was lodged at the National Maritime Museum.

To convey the period and environment in which this account unfolds, we have endeavoured to include contemporary images of the vessels, places and people. Unearthing old photographs is often a rewarding task though frequently spanning many months, sometimes even years. Getting consent for use can add even more time and, just occasionally, that permission is not forthcoming. Against that background we must give a special thanks to the Hull Daily Mail who were e-mailed seeking a period image of the Eagle Oil Mills there. The email was answered by James Mitchell, the paper's Picture Editor, together with a high resolution scan of a suitable image and the necessary consent, just 34 minutes later!

Our colleagues of the S.S.B.R. have had their input, in particular the Society's Chairman Emeritus Tony Farnham; Secretary John White; members including ex. bargeman Ray Rush; Newport, I.O.W. Harbour Master Wayne Pritchett; Ron Green and Tony Millatt at Mersea Island Museum; artist Robert Dennis; Richard and Joan Smith; John Ritchie at Books Afloat, Weymouth and Greenhithe historian David Challis. Thanks go to Mike Sparkes of the Norfolk Wherry Trust; Sheila Hutchinson and John Baker, Hugh Muir from Corpach and Susan Butler who has the good fortune to live in a cottage just 20 feet from the River Ouse.

Waterways enthusiast Alan Faulkner; Blue Circle archivist John Oxford; Director of B.O.C.M. Pauls, Nick Major; Willie Wilson, M.D. of chart publishers Imray, Laurie, Norie & Wilson; British Sugar plc archivist Steve Cash; all these and more have gone the extra mile to help fulfil the Fielder project.

Quite a lot of photographs have come from overseas; thanks to Simon Bang in Copenhagen for his image of Kattendijk Locks, Antwerp; Roger Wilmut for his Ijmuiden sea lock photo; but of all who have helped from across the sea there can be none more worthy of praise than Rob Hoogenbos who, in addition to many Dutch newspaper cuttings about her, has located more photos of *Prowess* in the waterways of The Netherlands than the rest of us have found of her in U.K. waters! As a result we thank for the help of Saskia van Bavel at Bergen op Zoom and Dirk Ronitz at the Municipal Archives at Zaanstad.

David Wood
Richard Walsh

INTRODUCTION

Charles Henry Fielder, was according to his niece Glynis Feichtlbauer, "... on the barges all his life". Indeed she understands all the Fielder family, including his brothers George and Harry, worked on the river in one capacity or another all their lives. Charlie Fielder's home was at Riverside Gardens, Hammersmith, W.6., a block of flats now to the north of the Cromwell Road extension on the east side of the Town Hall, but he was destined to work far from his home there at the head of Hammersmith Creek.

Following his death in 1993, Glynis obtained her uncle's papers and in 2008 deposited them with the Twickenham Museum. The 'Fielder Archive' includes a quarto size red exercise book which contains a hand-written diary, virtually a log of his time spent on the vessels in which he served, first the sailing barges, and later the ships, owned by F.T. Everard & Sons Ltd. The archive includes the 'Chief Officers Log Book' of the motor tanker *Prowess*, from the date of her commissioning in 1926, supplemented by five 'scrap' Boots scribbling diaries for 1933 - 1937 completed as the 'Deck Logbook', and a mass of books, pamphlets, and ephemera listed in Appendix V.

This narrative follows in some detail the lives of both the people - Charlie himself, his close family and working colleagues - and the craft aboard which he served; also of those other vessels which impacted, sometimes literally, upon them.

His was not a life untouched by tragedy, a factor which no doubt steered his career, as the reader will come to realise whilst Charlie's working life unfolds within these pages.

David G Wood

FOREWORD

The origins of our family business date back to the late 1800s when wind was the predominant power for the coastal trade,

Over sixty sailing barges were owned by Everard, including a number of the larger ones built by the firm at its Greenhithe yard and later by Fellows at Great Yarmouth, a shipyard in which Everard took a controlling interest.

During W.W.I the first motor ship, a ground-breaking design, though still retaining a sailplan, was launched at Greenhithe into the Thames. Although some steam powered coasters were later added to the fleet, there was growing preference for the progressively more cost effective 'oil engine' motor ship which, 100 years later, in its present guise is still a mainstay of cargo shipping around the world.

Despite the austerity after the Great War and the crippling slump of the late '20s, the Everard business, formalised as F.T. Everard & Sons Ltd. in 1922, continued to prosper, no less than 70 vessels joining the fleet during the inter-war years.

This was a period of rapid change and development. It was into this environment that Charles Henry Fielder came when he joined one of the company's sailing barges in December 1919. It was a career move which was to take him though sail and steam to the motorships, one of which he went on to command.

Within these pages the fascinating details of the trades, ships, crews and cargoes, gathered from Charlie Fielder's records and never before detailed in print, paint a unique picture of an era already beyond the memory and imagination of today's seafarers.

F. Michael Everard C.B.E.

Loading 2 cwt.
sacks of cement
(over 100 kilos!)
into barges at
Holborough Works.

Charles Henry Fielder always maintained he was born on 31st August, 1903; but he didn't have a birth certificate to prove it. His niece, Glynis Feichtlbauer, who visited her 'Uncle Charlie' daily in his later years recalls him strenuously maintaining that he was a 'Man of Kent' and had been baptised in Rochester Cathedral. There are, however, no records that confirm this.

Long after he retired Charlie wrote about his family to the Editor of Coast & Country magazine. 'My family have been bargemen for generations. When I was a little boy away with father in his barge, I saw the remains of the *Graphic* in Lee's old dock at Halling submerged in silt. His father had been skipper of her and had placed her there as she had been condemned by the insurance company as being unfit to carry lime cargoes.'

The records of The Company of Watermen & Lightermen of the River Thames does indeed show Fielders being bound apprentices from 1706, but many members of the family lived and worked on the Medway. Charlie's grandfather Henry and his wife, Emma May were, in 1871, living at 4, (now 10) East Street, Snodland, a couple of miles from Halling, about five miles upstream of Chatham on the Medway. The 40 ton *Graphic* of Rochester had been built in 1876 for Samuel Lee Smith of Halling who had just joined the board of cement makers Lee, Son & Smith.

The firm became William Lee, Son & Co. Ltd. and Smith's black sailed barges, many stumpie rigged, swim headed and tiller steered were successful in the early sailing barge matches. They were, it was said, treated like yachts, never overloaded or rough handled, being brightly painted, with black hulls, grey transom and rails, red ochre deck dressing, and a blue sprit, the sling painted with bands of red - white - yellow - white - red, with the barge's name and port of registry done in gold-leaf. The firm built up a fleet of over thirty vessels but went into liquidation in 1912. Lees were one of the 33 companies acquired by British Portland Cement Manufacturers Ltd., a subsidiary of A.P.C.M. in 1931 and were shut down as a direct result of the competition created by the installation of new technology at the Holborough cement works.

Henry and Emma May had at least four sons; Henry born c.1868, William J. born 1872, Charles (Charlie's father), born 28th April 1874 and Alfred born 1878. By 1881 the family had moved to 9, Poynder Terrace, Halling, at which date *Graphic* was crewed by two members of the Fielder clan. Her master was Thomas Fielder of Ightham Mote born in 1842 with, as mate, Richard, born in 1832, who had been 'in service' and lived in Holborough Road, Snodland. As might be expected, Capt. Henry Fielder's sons followed their father, living and working on their barges. Henry, the eldest, was mate on Lee's barge, the 38 ton *Renown* under John H. Aldridge with Percy Aldridge as 'the boy', recorded in Bow Creek, West Ham, during the 1891 census.

The bawley *Thistle*, constructed by Gill at Rochester in 1887, towing her trawl under topsail and foresail, with her loose-footed mainsail brailed up.

On Christmas Day, 1899, Capt. Henry Fielder's bargeman son Charles, aged 27, married Rebecca Pocock aged 21, spinster, in St. Mary's Church, Chatham. The bridegroom's brother Alfred was best man and both bride and groom gave their home address as being 1, Medway Street, Chatham, the riverside road near the Sun Pier. Rebecca almost certainly went away with Charles early in their marriage as much later their son Charles Henry wrote 'My mother could sail a barge as well as any man. My maternal grandfather was a fisherman owning boats in Chatham and had the bawley *Thistle* built for him. Her lowering mast, like a barge's, was so that she could get under Rochester Bridge to Halling and Wouldham for the smelt fishing season there. He lived at 1, Medway Street, Chatham close to Arthur Gamman's[1] Holborn Wharf and died in 1914 at the age of 86, being interred in Chatham Cemetery with his headstone being in the design of a fouled anchor. My uncle 'Masher' Pocock sailed the craft which cost about £600 when new, and my uncle, Tom Pocock, claimed to have seen a sea serpent in the Medway.'

Rebecca gave birth to Doreen, who was three months old when the Census of 1901 was taken. Rebecca and her daughter were then living with her father, George Pocock, aged 66, and his brother, Thomas, aged 68, at 1, Medway Street. They were both fishermen,

Chatham bawleys in Victorian times, the Chatham Rowing Club (founded 1869) has its raft with boat store in the middle distance, the Naval Dockyard beyond.

as was Rebecca's brother Henry, then aged 18, who was also living at the family home. Doreen's grandparents, Capt. Henry and Emma Fielder had moved to 76, Grove Road, Frindsbury, but the only children still living with them were Thomas, aged 19, and Emma May, a draper's apprentice, aged 15, both born in Halling. By this time Capt. Charles and his brother Alfred, were master and mate of Sankey & Co.'s Regent's Canal size barge, the 42 ton *Willie*. Later they were working together on Sankey's new similar sized *Cecil* sailing between the Medway and the Thames.

At the time of the 1911 census, the brothers were on board the *Cecil*, with their father Henry then aged 70, listed, on this occasion, as a passenger. Rebecca and her children were still living in Chatham, having moved to 31, Fort Pitt Street, a road running south from the railway station in the Ordnance Place area of the town. Her daughter Doreen, then aged 10 was apparently staying with her grandmother, Emma May and aunt May in Frindsbury, but living with Rebecca were her son Charles Henry (Charlie), then aged 8, and his brothers James Alfred, aged 6, George, aged 3 and 18 month old Henry Thomas (Harry) all of whom the census records as being born in Rochester. Rebecca had been designated 'head of the household' while the records stated that of her seven children, five were alive and two had died. The family were to grow with the addition of Gordon, sister Emily and Walter John (Wally).

By June 1915 Capt. Charles Fielder gave his home address on the half yearly Crew List for S.B. *Cecil* as 12, Grange Road, Strood, but he had only been employed in the River Thames above Gravesend. By this time his brother Alfred was no longer mate, having being replaced by 15 year old John Brown who had previously worked ashore. The barge was being managed by Wm. S. Such, a city shipbroker.

Beyond his comments about the *Graphic*, Charlie gave little information about his time away with his father, but in his letters to Coast & Country he does relate some of his life before he started to record his activities himself:

'I was a boy third hand in Samuel West's barge *Mystery*, and anchored close to the wreck of the boomie barge *Olympia* on several occasions, the remains of which were later dispersed by explosives; George Douglas[2] who much later was to be my skipper in the M.V. *Prowess*, had been mate of the barge at the time.

'During the 1914-18 First World War I served as mate in the sailing barge *H. Pierrepoint* when she was owned by a family at Greenhithe by the name of Eales, who also owned the *Alfred*, *Snipe* and *William*. On the death of Mr. Eales the *H. Pierrepoint*[3] was sold to 'Black Jack' Rayfield of Northfleet who I believe was her master when she was lost loaded with lead spelter. While I was employed by A.P.C.M. I was mate of the *Black Duck*, Capt. Stevens, and the *J.M.W.*, Capt. W. Collins.'

The first mention of the Greenhithe barge builders and owners, F.T. Everard & Sons Ltd., or their barges, occurs in a letter to East Coast Digest as the magazine Coast & Country had been renamed.

[2] George Douglas's brother was also master in Everard ships and they used to relieve each other.
[3] The sailing barge *H. Pierrepoint* was recorded in the 1917 MNL as belonging to Eales, but by 1919 was owned by Smy, possibly with Rayfield as master.

'I sailed with Tommy Dike in S.B. *Britisher* as third hand for £1 a week and grub, between December 1919 and 1922. Tom kept his cargo book in an old ditty box in his state room. He was well known in many continental ports and his clothing was mainly bought over on the other side. He would wear Dutch fisherman's knicker-bockers and clogs and a soft peaked cap. Tommy, as I knew him was completely bald and clean shaven wearing big gold rings in his ears. I can remember his old accordion on which he used to play before turning in. Nobody could teach him anything about coasting and he was one of the very few skippers who could navigate the Gore[4] in the dark. He also knew where the oyster beds were and although there was a Watch Boat off Whitstable, he would tow a dredge and get some up for us.

Britisher unloads a cargo of bagged grain at Gleadell's Mills, Morton Corner, River Trent.

'We were in the first fleet of Thames barges to arrive at Antwerp after the war. I made many voyages in her, several from Goole to

Antwerp via the Hanswert and Wemeldinge Canal to the small fishing port of Yerikse to load oyster shells for River Head, Grimsby. Then we went from Goole to Shoreham, Northam and Guernsey to Faversham. That trip I remember very well as it was on the occasion of the heavyweight contest between Carpentier and Jack Dempsey in July 1921. The passage was rather unique.

[4] The Gore Channel lies between Margate Hook and the north Kent coast.

We left St. Sampsons C.I. and had wind enough to pass us through the Little Russel[5]. Then it dropped a flat calm and we got into a whirlpool of tide at the Casquets[6], which nearly ended us on the rocks. In all we were ten days on passage.

'The last trips I made with Tommy before going mate of the *Agnes Mary* were from London to King's Lynn, thence to Goole to load for Shoreham, from Shoreham to Boulogne, then to Clark's Wharf Erith for Tunnel Cement to Hammersmith.

'When I left the *Britisher* and joined the *Agnes Mary* under Fred Bailey a picture of myself at the age of about 18 or 19 was taken in Gorleston when we were loaded with a freight of Wincarnis for Barking Creek. We had previously taken port wine from London Dock to Norwich and this was the return cargo. Later I

Charlie Fielder by the wheel of the *Agnes Mary*, when about 18 years old.

served in S.B. *Briton* which, if my memory serves me correctly, was lost north of Wells while attempting to pass through the swatchway known as the Woolpack, avoiding the N.E. Docking shoal. By the time the Wells lifeboat arrived the barge had sunk but some of the mast still showed above water and the crew were rescued from the rigging.'

5. Little Russel is a channel between Herm and Guernsey, in the Channel Islands.
6. The Casquets are notorious rocks N.W. of Alderney, guarded by a lighthouse, the first erected in 1724.

The earliest documentary record that Charlie Fielder himself kept was his 1920 contribution card No.11647, issued to him by the Amalgamated Society of Watermen, Lightermen, Tugmen and Bargemen's Union when he was aged 17. The card for the quarter to December, 1920 shows arrears of contributions on a previous card of 2/- (10p) and a contribution of 8/6d (43p) made on 4th October, 1920. There are later contribution cards for the period from 1937/8 until 1947/8 to the Watermen, Lightermen, Tugmen & Bargemen's Union, but until this time Charlie had spent his time on sailing barges working for their skippers. In 1924 he joined the staff of F.T. Everard & Sons Ltd., one of his first jobs that year as temporary mate of the big 1897 built swimhead barge *Gerty* for two or three freights.

The firm had been started by Frederick T. Eberhardt who had himself worked as a barge builder for Alfred Keep at Battersea. He moved to Keep's yard at Greenhithe, becoming the foreman

Built in 1894 at Sandwich by Wm. Felton, *Agnes Mary* came into Everard ownership in 1919. The picture shows mail being delivered aboard by a postman afloat.

shipwright and by 1880 had acquired the yard himself. Within a decade he began to trade with sailing barges on his own account and accepted many innovations including in 1913 with the auxiliary ketch *Grit*, the installation of an engine in a wooden sailing barge hull in the course of its construction by Everard to his own account. He changed his name by deed poll during the 1914-18 War and her successor, the sail assisted wooden motor-barge, *Grit*, built in 1923, led to the development of the steel coastal motorship, although he had to look elsewhere for yards to build them. In 1922 F.T. Everard & Sons Ltd. was formed and in a letter to Coast & Country magazine in August, 1978, Charlie wrote 'I served my time under the founder of Everards. They were a very clever family, all of them well qualified; Mr. Will was a shipwright; Mr. Fred was a shipwright and marine surveyor; Mr. Alf was a Chief Engineer and Miss Ethel an accountant. Mr. Will had served his time as a

chippy in H.M.S. *Ceres* during the First World War and, when he was demobbed, many of his naval pals found jobs with the firm. In the old City office, which was later bombed, he had a large picture of this ship and also of one of the first coastal cargo ships that they owned, the *Tosca*. I joined her as an A.B. in

H.M.S. *Ceres* in Malta, c.1920.

1924 and was later promoted bosun and then second mate under Capt. J.R. MacDonald.'

According to Ken Garrett, who was F.T. Everard & Sons' Marine Superintendent, before becoming Marine Director,

from 1970 to 1998, writing in Everard of Greenhithe states that the 449 grt. *Tosca* was one of three small dry cargo steam ships that were acquired by the Greenhithe barge builder and owner during the First World War. The other craft, *Norseman* and *Bellavale* were sold by 1920. Following the

The steamer *Tosca*, centre, built at Ayr in 1908, was torpedoed and sunk by a Royal Navy submarine during W.W.II when in Italian ownership.

formation of F.T. Everard & Sons Ltd., *Tosca* was transferred to the company by its founder.

Steamships, motor vessels and sailing barges were registered as British Ships under the series of Navigation Acts dating from 1660 and appeared in the annual Mercantile Navy Lists. However, many of the sailing barges and the numerous lighters or dumb barges were registered under another system which goes back to the period when the river from the Nore to Staines was administered by the Corporation of the

The Greenhithe shipyard of F.T. Everard & Sons Ltd. in 1947. Nearest the sheds is the second *Actuality*, built in 1945, replacing her namesake mined in 1940. Outside her is the second *Anonity*, a tanker, previously the *Empire Campden*, recently arrived from the Ministry of Transport, her earlier namesake also mined. Left of picture is the 89 feet long, 1916 built, *Annuity*, the shore end of the trot occupied by the tank barge *Southward*.

City of London. Those who worked aboard them were governed by The Company of Watermen and Lightermen of the River Thames. Sometime before 1803 the City Company had begun to list their members who owned barges and lighters and from 1859 they were required by law to list the names of 'persons keeping boats for carrying goods'. The Thames Conservancy was formed in 1857 to take over the administration of the river from the City and started the series of Registers which are now held in the Museum in Docklands. However, the Watermen's Company continued to administer the registration of craft on behalf of the authorities until long after the Port of London Authority took over from the Conservancy on 31st March, 1909.

A distinctive number was issued to each owner who was obliged to paint his name with that of the craft on the stern of his lighters and sailing barges. The Owner Number 1771 was allocated to Frederick T. Eberhardt of 1, Forrest Terrace, Greenhithe, when in 1897 he was registered as owner of the sailing barges *Industry* and *Despatch*. On 12th April 1900 he registered the *Prompt*, *Lord Kitchener*, and *Energy* and in ensuing years, the *Elizabeth*, *Alert*, *Hilda*, *Scot* and *Pride of the Colne*, and probably others, were added to the navigation authority's register. The smallest class of tank lighters registered by the firm in the period that Charlie was employed were the stem-headed canal barges fitted with tanks with a burden tonnage of 58¾, steel built, 76' x 12'8" x 4'3". This class included the hatched barges *Diamond*, *Pearl*, *Ruby*, *Emerald* and *Sapphire* built 1925/6 and the open barges, *Lea* P.L.A. Barge No. 12491, *Brent* No. 12492, registered 2nd June 1926 and *Dart* No. 13237 registered 23rd September 1926. The company owned three classes of tank river barges, the smallest with a burden tonnage of 174¾, were 85' x 22'5" x 6'11" which had been built during 1932/3 and included *Dogwatch*, *Portwatch*, *Middlewatch*, *Morningwatch*, *Nightwatch* and *Starboardwatch*. The second class, with a burden tonnage of 175¼, were 87' x 21'4" x 7'0"; *Eastward*, *Northward*, *Southward*, *Westward*, *Leeward*, *Windward*. The largest class, with a burden tonnage of 186, were 86' x 23'2" x 7'0" included *Inward*, *Outward* and *Upward*, many of which were to be mentioned in the logbooks kept on board the company's ships.

In January 1924 *Tosca* had been taken into a shipyard in Great Yarmouth, almost certainly the Fellows' yard, for repair and refit which included a new windlass, propeller and hold ceiling. While this work was going on it seems Charlie took work elsewhere and was at the Pier Hotel, presumably the hotel by Greenhithe Causeway. On 20th January 1924, Captain J.R. MacDonald, wrote to him from Great Yarmouth reporting on the progress made in the refit. He asked to be remembered to a Mr. Goodwin[7] saying he was sorry to hear of the death of Mr. Coker's son[8]. He also mentioned that Rory Munrow, the mate, was about to be married to a young lady from Norwich. But of more importance to Charlie was the news that the firm's managing director's sons, Mr. William and Mr. Fred had gone up to Great Yarmouth to inspect the ship (and the crew). From what Capt. MacDonald was able to report, the Directors had decided they would be keeping Charlie Fielder working 'on the river' for them. Perhaps this was the incentive for the 21 year old Fielder to start his red exercise book giving details of his work day-by-day.

The book starts on 23rd April 1924 with *Tosca* having finished loading at Rochester at 5 p.m., taking a Pilot onboard to proceed

[7.] Jack Goodwin was Everard's lighterage foreman. His son, also Jack, took over the role, retiring c.1990.
[8.] Captain Coker had other sons; Eric became foreman electrician, Cecil foreman shipwright.

Charlie's 'log' of the S.S *Tosca* from 23rd April 1924

on voyage to Middlesbrough. The successive changes in her course during the night on passage to Tees Bay, where they anchored to await the tide on 25th April, were duly noted. At 4.40 a.m. they hove up the anchor to proceed into port, take on a Pilot and moor at Casebourne's Cement wharf at Haverton Hill ready to commence discharging at 7 a.m. The forehatch was finished at 6 p.m., after which they started on the after hatch working until 8 p.m. when the day's work was finished. The crew started work at 7 a.m. next morning to finish at 6 p.m. in heavy rain.

The following day, 27th April was a Sunday so the crew were off duty for the day. Work started at 6 a.m. on Monday and the cargo was discharged in a couple of hours, after which the Pilot came on board to shift the ship alongside the coal hoist. By

21

10.45 a.m. they had been bunkered and set off, dropping the Pilot and steaming all day to find a safe anchorage, which was reached just after midnight off Dysart, a small port just north of Kirkcaldy on the Firth of Forth. Anchor watch was kept all night and in the morning a Pilot took them into the docks to load. Finished by 2.20 p.m. on 1st May, the hatches battened down, the Pilot came back aboard and they proceeded on the return voyage to London. The passage was uneventful save for the sighting of H.M.S. *Ramilles* bound to Rosyth, Scotland. They dropped anchor off the Powder Jetty at Higham Bight, in the lower Thames. At 1 a.m. on 4th May, they were to proceed to the Harrison Jetty in the Victoria Docks and spend the next day unloading.

Tosca locked out to anchor off Greenhithe for stores with orders to proceed to Rochester buoys to load. The cargo, presumably cement, was again for the Tees River, where they berthed at Haverton Hill Cement Works for a day of rest on Sunday 11th May. After unloading they set off north to Burntisland Docks, just six miles south of Dysart, to load for Harrison's Jetty again. The next cargo was for the Humber Docks, where there was a hold up as a winch rod broke at noon on Saturday. The freight of basic slag was for Southampton where they moored on Wednesday 28th May. A crane ran off its rails which held up unloading but they sailed light for

Burntisland Docks on the north side of the Forth Estuary.

Guernsey in fine weather on Saturday afternoon. The cargo loaded was stone for Rochester but there was no berth available when they arrived, so they moored on buoys until Cory's were free.

Back on the buoys to await the next job, orders came to load more cement for the River Tees where unloading was interrupted by heavy rain, not a happy bed-fellow of cement!

The rain continued next day, but between the worst of it the discharge was completed. The weather further deteriorated with a very strong gale of wind from the north-east. This and heavy seas running meant *Tosca* was making no headway as she attempted to get north. It was not until 5 p.m. that they arrived off Dysart to anchor and send the boat for orders. A berth was available and *Tosca* loaded for London. On arrival she discharged, took on bunkers, and started to load another rain-interrupted cement cargo. It was not until 6.30 p.m. next day that they were able to leave to pick up the sailing barge *Lord Kitchener* at Swanscombe to tow her as far as Spurn Head, where they turned into the Humber, up past Hull into the River Ouse to load at Goole.

From Goole Docks, they had to wait at Blacktoft Jetty, above the merging of the Ouse with the River Trent, for water over Whitton Sands. When they had water it was full-speed for Littlehampton. Spurn Point was passed at 4.45 p.m. next day, the day after the South Foreland was abeam at 12.20 p.m., Beachy Head by 5.30 p.m. then to anchor off, to await the tide

Blacktoft Jetty, with its distinctive look-out tower used to get early information on approaching vessels.

and Pilot to the Coal Wharf at Littlehampton. *Tosca* was then off to Guernsey, light, to load stone for Lowestoft followed by Goole for freight and bunkering to repeat the previous passage, this time the stone was for Angerstein Wharf, Greenwich and Johnson's Wharf, Greenhithe. The diary continues on including 26th June 1924 when *Tosca* loaded at Dysart for London, the entries ending abruptly the next day at 4.30 p.m. abeam the Longstone Light.

The diary does not name his fellow crew members but in the April 1979 issue of Coast & Country Charlie recalled in response to a letter asking about a skipper who shouted out 'Happy days' when passing another barge, confirmed that it was Albert Fever, adding that 'In 1924 Albert sailed with me when I was second mate in the steamer *Tosca* and was in my watch. He had lived at Strood and I had known him from childhood when I was away with my father on his barge. He was a very happy-go-lucky sort of man and had the handicap of a withered arm. Many years later, during the Second World War, there was a press report that when he was skipper of Sales' barge *Crow*[9] he was run over by a locomotive at the Royal Arsenal, Woolwich.'

The next page of the exercise book, recommences the 'log' and records *Tosca* sailing light from Great Yarmouth to Goole on 20th February 1925 to load coal for Guernsey, returning in ballast on 23rd for another cargo. It continues until on 23rd April 1925 when *Tosca* sailed for Middlesbrough at 3 a.m., mooring at Tyne & Tees Wharf to commence discharging both hatches at 10.45 a.m., and to cover the forehatch followed by aft hatch at 5.45 p.m. and commence bunkering 50 tons of coal. There the log ends.

The Crew List held at the National Maritime Museum at Greenwich shows that *Tosca* was under repair from 27th April until the 6th May, 1925, with Capt. MacDonald being transferred to another command on 19th May while the first engineer, Wm.J. Cane, age 45, of Gillingham, was transferred on 30th May. The second engineer, G. Lucking, 56, of London; the mate, 30 year old D. Munro of Wick; second mate, C.H. Fielder, 21, of Chatham; able seamen V.C. Beckett, 47, and J. Baday, 20, along with ordinary seaman C. Tomlinson, 16, and the fireman, W. Case, 20, from Goole and D.H. Wilson, 22, from Hull, were all transferred or discharged on 6th June. The list also discloses the pay of each member of the crew; the captain receiving the weekly sum of £7.10s.0d., the mate £4.10s.0d., second mate £4.0s.0d., able seamen £3.8s.6d., ordinary seamen £2.5s.0d., whilst the first engineer received £5.0s.0d. and his second £4.10s.0d. with £3.8s.6d. being paid to the firemen.

While *Tosca* was under repair Charlie Fielder was posted to the steam tanker *Agility*. She was the first of such craft to be built

[9]. The sailing barge *Crow* was, according to the MNL of the time referred to in the text, belonging to H.R. Mitchell of Woolwich; the 'press report' was probably incorrect as to ownership.

The steam tanker *Agility* built on the Clyde in 1924, the first of the Everard fleet to be named with the 'ity' suffix.

for the Company by George Brown & Co. at their Garvel Shipyard at Greenock in 1924. It seems that W.J.(Bill) Everard had formed a link with the shipbuilders during his service in the Royal Navy in the First World War when, as Ken Garrett reports, 'Bill' had stated he intended to build a dozen vessels. In fact she was the first of twenty-eight craft and the first to be named with the 'ity' suffix.

There had been quite a turnover in her crew during her first years with the company; G. Whitney-Dimes and A. Hadlow being in command in addition to John MacDonald who was appointed master on 20th May, 1925, when she sailed light from London to Hull. She delivered a cargo to Schiedam on 23rd, sailing with water ballast on 25th to Hamburg, a passage repeated several times. Charlie joined the ship on 18th June for a trip from London to Vlaardingen, loading there on 20th June, but not being discharged in Hull until 11th July. The second of the half-yearly returns mentions an incident at 10.20 a.m. on 19th November 1925 while discharging motor sprit in the basin at Preston Dock. The tops of both No.1 port and starboard tanks were blown off, killing two and injuring five members of the crew; including the then master William Miller, the engineer James Tierney, and H.E. Williams all of whom were taken to Preston Infirmary and later discharged. Those killed were the chief officer, Frederick Lawrence, age 24, and Able seaman

Ashton Hunt. No explanation of the cause of the accident could be given in the master's report at the time, but much later, in writing about the Petroleum Regulations which he first encountered on this ship, Charlie Fielder commented that 'Rules were altered after an explosion aboard a tanker of Everards, the *Agility*, in which two hands were killed. The two men were friends of mine, strange to say sometime previously I had been relief second mate of her. It was said at the enquiry that it was believed to be caused by a scratch in the insulating cover which exposed a minute bit of wire. The wire was attached to the light clusters they had to lower down in the tank to see how much petrol was in the tank. I had the unpleasant job of breaking the news to Hunt's brother, who was our cook in the *Tosca*, when we were laying at Plymouth.'

The repairs to *Tosca* were apparently completed on 19th May 1925 when forty year old Capt. A. Hadlow of Rochester was appointed her Master. He had previously been serving on the sailing barge *Hibernia* and took command of the steamer for the passage from London to West Hartlepool on 21st May, Middlesbrough by 25th, at Queenborough on the Swale in Kent 27th to 29th (presumably unloading) and returning to London (Greenhithe) were she remained under repair, again, from 30th May until the end of the first half-yearly return for 1925. In fact, the ship remained on the yard until 23rd July 1925, when Capt. C. Coker from the motor tanker *Wander* was appointed master with as mate W.J. Farnes, aged 28, from Everard's auxiliary schooner *Capable* which was converted that year to a fully powered motor vessel. Charlie Fielder returned as 2nd mate with C.G. Hunt, 20, also from *Agility*, who was able

The big spritsail coaster *Hibernia*, built by Everard in 1906, seen here at West Bay, Dorset.

seaman along with the appropriately named R.R. Seaman, 25, from the ketch barge *Martinet*. The ordinary seaman was H. Dibsdall, aged 20, from the S.B. *Agnes Mary* which had been regularly working between Colchester, Yarmouth and Lowestoft in addition to her regular cement freights from the Tunnel Works on the Thames at Thurrock, under her then master, R. Pringle of Chatham. The first engineer was G. Lucking while C.A. Burgess, aged 25, from Dartford, signed on as his No.2 with W. Stevens, 49, and J.A. Ryan, aged 54 as stokers and firemen.

Within days there appears to have been an incident leading to the suspension of the master and mate on 1st August 1925, with all the crew being discharged on 9th August. Putting a new crew aboard *Tosca* included the re-appointment of Capt. A. Hadlow as master 'on an agreement', a post that was to last until 17th October. He was joined by another Hadlow, a lady aged 39 appointed as 'stewardess' at £2 a week, she also having previously served aboard the sailorman, *Hibernia*. W.J. Case, 45, from the steam tanker *Alchymist*, signed on as first engineer with G. Lucking as his No.2. Munro returned as first mate but while Charlie Fielder remained in the crew, he was described as Bosun being paid £3.13s.6d. a week for the passage to Rochester on 12th August, to load for Southampton.

However, the suspended Capt. C. Coker returned to his command and in due course completed the second half-yearly return showing some 14 passages from London to Plymouth or Southampton, proceeding in ballast (water) to Guernsey before returning to London. The Registrar of Shipping had picked up a discrepancy, as there appeared to be two masters for the period from 19th September to 17th October, but Capt. Coker corrected the mistake, as he had not resumed command until later.

Tosca, a familiar sight in the waters around Southampton was sold to W.A.Wilson there in 1926, when Everard bought the slightly larger, 650 ton, dry-cargo collier, S.S. *Tirydail* in which Charlie Fielder was also to serve. The red notebook is blank until a page lists stores bought at Millwall, Greenhithe and Southend, followed by a brief summary of hours worked

The steam collier *Tirydail*, with central bridge island and well-deck forward. A proper little ship.

aboard the *Tirydail* loading cement on 10th January 1927, before details of the passage to Exmouth, where they started to discharge their cargo on Friday 14th. They resumed work at 7.30 a.m. on Saturday, finishing at 4.30 p.m., when they proceeded towards Plymouth, covering up the hatches in clear weather as they went. Charlie Fielder relieved the mate at the wheel until they arrived at Cattedown, Plymouth, to anchor at 11.46 p.m. On Sunday the anchor was weighed and they moored alongside at Coles Wharf to start discharging the rest of the cement on Monday 17th January, 1927.

Tunnel Wharf at West Thurrock Marshes, where raw materials for cement manufacture were delivered and the finished product shipped away by sailing barge.

Charlie Fielder records his joining the 73 grt. sailing barge *Hilda* at Greenhithe on 24th March 1927 and his discharge from the barge on 17th October, 1928. The notebook does not say if he was her Master, listing only the loading berth, usually Tunnel Works, the date, the cargo recorded as the number of casks loaded, without expressing their contents. There is no doubting it was cement, as this was one way it was carried before the days of hessian sacks and, much later, paper bags. The diary also names the ship being loaded and date of discharge, usually in one or other of the enclosed docks in London.

After discharging 500 casks aboard a ship in the Victoria Dock on 27th August, *Hilda* returned next day to Everard's wharf at Greenhithe for general repairs and to have the sails overhauled, dressed, etc. She left the yard on Monday 17th September to return to Tunnel Works to load yet again. The last pencil hand-written note is of loading 518 casks for the Brocklebank S.S. *Mahout* on 8th October, and their discharge into her six days later.

Clyde-built in 1925, *Mahout* survived W.W.II, to be scrapped at Blyth in 1961.

This was not to be his last trading under sail but Charlie Fielder must have seen that his future lay with the motor ships owned by F.T. Everard & Sons Limited. Nevertheless, he still had frequent meetings with the sailing barges they owned when the ships in which he served were instructed to take them in tow. And, of course, his father still worked in the 'sailormen'.

After the sale of *Cecil* to Wm. F. Tester of Pier Cottage, Greenhithe, in 1917, it seems that Charlie's father may have followed the barge there. *Cecil* was to remain in Tester's ownership until 23rd February 1932, when she was in collision with the S.S. *Lady Martin* off Wapping and sank.

Certainly in 1919 Capt. Fielder and Becky were staying in a flat at Woodlands, on the corner of Station Road and High Street, Greenhithe. Since 1952 the building has been Grade II listed by English Heritage as a building of historic significance, with its entrance porch with doric columns, decorated fanlight and cast iron handrails.

Built by Wm. Felton at Sandwich for the Margate Hoy Co. in 1895, the *John Bayly* came under the Everard flag in 1918.

It was here on 11th August, 1919 that their son Walter John (Wally) was born, the youngest of her twelve children. Some ninety years later Wally recalls "Our dad was always referred to as 'Ike' because he was so tight, but as skipper he did not get home often." When next recorded, his father was master of the Everard sailing barge *John Bayly* of Ramsgate (as confirmed by the Half Yearly Return made by the company in 1923) with his second son James Alfred as mate, trading in the Thames and Medway prior to taking command of their *Agnes Mary* on 27th August 1927.

CHAPTER II

Hammersmith Connections

In his Handbook to the Environs of London, published in 1876, James Thorne had referred to 'the once fashionable part of Hammersmith being divided into the Upper and Lower Mall by the Creek, a dirty inlet of the Thames which is crossed by a wooden foot-bridge, built originally by Bishop Sherlock in 1751 and known as the High Bridge; the region of squalid tenements bordering the Creek having acquired the cognomen of 'Little Wapping', probably from its confined and dirty character'.

Hammersmith Creek was a deep, narrow, not quite straight channel running 200 metres inland from the River Thames towards King Street where there was a stormwater outlet from the Stamford Brook. There were cottages on either side of its mouth and about a 30 metres up the creek was the old footbridge. On the

The entrance to Hammersmith Creek from the Thames, the footbridge necessitating the lowering of a barge's gear to get access to the wharves further up the creek.

west side of the creek were the malthouses of the Town Brewery founded by Thomas Cromwell around 1780 and on the east at Creek Wharf, the builders yard of the lime and cement merchants and barge owners, Sankey & Co. The Creek was only a short distance above the lowest bridge on the Thames tideway, nine miles above London Bridge, where the wharf had been run since 1884 by William George Martin Sankey of Borstal, near Rochester, and his partner, John Hunt Sankey.

Sankey & Co. were registered with the Thames Conservancy on 9th October 1895 as Barge Owner No. 1015 of the 30 foot sand punt *Fox*. They remained owners of the punt until well after the 1914-18 war, but although the Fielder brothers were master and mate on Sankey's sailing barge *Willie* in 1901, the firm had apparently not registered their ownership of the barge with the Conservancy. They did however, in 1912, belatedly register the *Cecil* and *Viola* in the name of William Sankey as Barge Owner No.1078. Both barges were 75 feet long, 14 feet wide and stumpie rigged, the annual registration fees payable to the newly established Port of London Authority were 19/- per annum for the 38 ton *Cecil* and 18/9d per annum for the 37½ ton *Viola*.

Sankey's *Cecil* pokes her way up the Creek to discharge her cargo. In 1917 *Cecil* was sold to W.F. Tester of Greenhithe.

Whilst Charlie's father was working for Sankey & Co. it must have seemed sensible for him to find accommodation for himself and his family near his employers place of business and according to family tradition Rebecca and her family came to live on a barge in the Creek. In 1917 the lease of the wharf was renewed for a further 30 years. Following the death of the partners, the business was taken over by Wiggins & Co. (Hammersmith) Ltd. to trade as Wiggins-Sankey Ltd. Nevertheless, the P.L.A. Monthly for November 1926, recorded traffic of 150 barges a year using the Creek, including the *Viola,* owned by Sankey, whose Skipper, Thomas Richard Wadhams, was a member of another well-known Medway barge family.

Gear raised to allow the cargo to be worked, a stumpie barge lies at Sankey's wharf.

Sankey's crane is swung to unload the barge's cargo at the head of the Creek. The mizzen mast has been left lowered, the hatch covers stacked ahead and astern of the main hatch. Being so narrow, the barges had to leave the Creek stern first after discharging.

It is not clear whether Charlie or his father was first to join the staff of F.T. Everard & Sons. Ltd. The company kept a record of their employees on a card index, the neatly typed cards gave details of each employee, the date of their appointment, their ship, status and the date of their departure. The card for C.H. Fielder has not survived although that for his father has. This records that Fielder, Charles, Snr., was employed on 27th August, 1927 as Captain of the *Agnes Mary*. The barge had been acquired by Miss Alice E. Everard in 1919 and the card gives as his previous command S.B. *John Bayly* which had been purchased by Alfred Everard in 1918.

Capt. Fielder Snr. remained with *Agnes Mary* for most of the rest of his life afloat with only a month, from 5th May 1931, on the firm's *Lady Marjorie*. Capt. Fielder would no doubt still be spending much of his time away on his barge but the electoral role for 1927/8 records Charles and Rebecca Fielder sharing No.1, South Street, Hammersmith with the long term residents Joseph and Christina Adams and Edward and Louise Gaish, while other residents included Ernest William and Mary Ann Fielder at 11, South Cottages; William and Amy Haysman at 6, New Street; and Mary Ann Owen sharing at 19, Waterloo Street. In the world of local government there were plans afoot which would affect them all.

The local council had begun to take an interest in the Creek area in 1917 when officials inspected the properties, house by house. They concluded that most were insanitary and incapable of improvement. In support of the proposal was a schedule showing death rates from disease in the area at almost twice that of the average for the Borough. A public inquiry in 1919 confirmed this view and in 1922 the Council began negotiations to acquire the land. In June, 1924 they published their proposals which were to include the demolition of some 100 residences as part of the Hammersmith Southern Improvement Scheme. This was promoted under the Housing Acts 'for the improvement of the area known as the Creek'. It was to take over ten years in all until, on 7th April 1927, the conveyance of the whole area to the Metropolitan Borough of Hammersmith was completed and compensation of £8,000 handed over to the various previous owners.

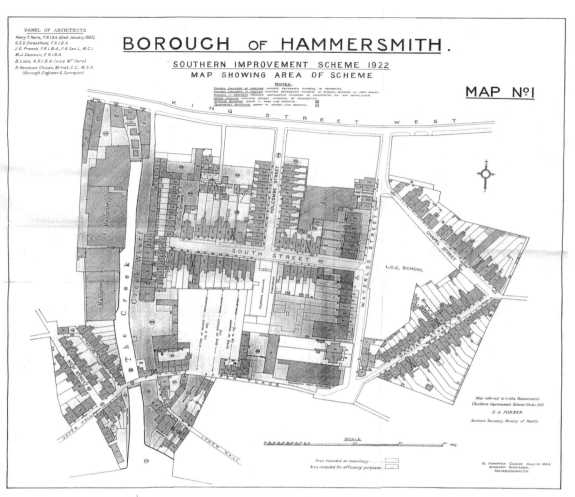

BOROUGH OF HAMMERSMITH.

SOUTHERN IMPROVEMENT SCHEME 1922
MAP SHOWING AREA OF SCHEME

MAP N°1

The plan of the area to the east of the Creek proposed for demolition and redevelopment to accommodate '1000 persons of the working classes'.

The Council's contractors, Wm. Walkerdine Limited, started building a three-story block of flats on 5th December 1928. The first phase comprised forty-eight four-bedroom, twenty-three three-bedroom, and ten two-bedroom flats, each with a separate living room, bathroom, lavatory and scullery with a central hot water supply. There was also a laundry and washhouse on the fourth floor. By 17th July 1929, eighty flats were under construction when the Council gave instructions for a further eighty-four to be put in hand and the name of Riverside Gardens was adopted for the whole development.

According to the Council, the buildings were 'to be far removed from the general type of tenements erected for the working classes, having more resemblance to the well known London square overlooking a large central garden area'. Almost as soon as the first phase of Riverside Gardens was completed Ada Edith Owen and her husband Thomas Frederick Owen with their young family moved into a new two-bedroom flat, No.73 in block H and started to pay the rent of fifteen shillings and nine pence a week. Mr. & Mrs. Owen were one of the first to benefit from the scheme which the Council considered would 'raise the Borough to a position of high rank in the community of boroughs, taking full advantage of the magnificent river frontage'.

The building of Riverside Gardens resulted in the demolition of all the old dwellings in South Street, Holcombe Street, Trafalgar Street and Waterloo Street (which was eventually renamed Macbeth Street), and the need to rehouse those who had been tenants there. Although the Sankey's Wharf and the malthouses of the Town Brewery on the opposite creekside were acquired by the Council, these were left outside the immediate development area, as were the houses in New Street to the west of the creek. This meant that William and Amy Haysman living in 6, New Street, their son William Junior and daughters Rosetta and Lily Elizabeth were not immediately affected. The Wharf itself was leased back to Wiggins & Co. (Hammersmith) Ltd. on 16th August 1929 and they continued trading as Wiggins-Sankey Ltd. until the lease was surrendered on 24th June 1931 when the business moved to an inland site.

A year or so after the first block of flats had been built and let, a further block containing flats 109 - 184 was completed. Charles Fielder Senior with his adult sons Charles Henry, George and Henry Thomas were allocated Flat No.110. Presumably James Alfred had a home elsewhere while Gordon, Emily and Wally were under age and would not be mentioned on the electoral role. William, Louie and Cecil Wadhams from No.2, The Creek, were also rehoused as were the residents of South Street where only Numbers 1 and 13 remained. The housing 'scheme' was by no means the only plan to affect the area; proposals were, in 1928, already under consideration for an extension of the Cromwell Road to join the Great West Road, while the idea of filling in the creek was mooted in July 1932, following which there was much public pressure for a park to be laid out alongside the Thames.

Whilst his parents found a home in Hammersmith, young Charlie Fielder joined the M.V. *Amenity* as mate on Wednesday 17th October 1928, under Capt. Fred Bailey who had been his skipper in the *Agnes Mary* and *Briton*. The two masted, engine aft, general cargo motorship *Amenity* had been built for the company in July 1928 and at 115 foot long with a beam of 23.2 feet was somewhat smaller than his previous coasters. On Thursday 18th October, with his new ship off Swanscombe Buoys, the compass was adjusted and the engine fired up and run on trial. After getting in the ships stores, they left Greenhithe at 5.25 p.m. to proceed on passage to Dungeness.

It was not an easy trip. They dropped anchor in 15 fathoms off the Middle Blyth Buoy in a strong south-westerly wind. On Friday they weighed anchor at 4.15 a.m., but encountered engine trouble and anchored in Margate Roads four hours later. After eight hours they weighed anchor again to proceed into the Downs to drop anchor in Deal Roads. The engine was still giving trouble, so anchor watches were kept all night.

Saturday was also spent weather-bound in a south-westerly gale, but they got under way at 5.55 a.m. on Sunday although they had to turn back three hours later to anchor in Dover Harbour. Monday morning was spent with trial running of the engine, now with an aft anchor out on 30 fathoms and a gale of wind. Next day the wind had moderated, the anchors weighed at 3.10 p.m. and at last, after three hours

Charlie's log recording his first days aboard the Amenity. Despite being brand new, she proved to be particularly difficult to steer when loaded. She was lost after striking a mine off the Humber in 1940.

37

underway they anchored in Dungeness East Bay with anchor watches being kept. On Wednesday they waited until 6.55 p.m. to attempt to berth, but the strong westerly wind and heavy sea made them turn back around midnight. The last entry in the book was made on Thursday 25th October 1928 at anchor off Dungeness with 30 fathoms of cable out, but he was to remain with Capt. Bailey for some further time although this is unrecorded in the notebook.

Built as the auxiliary two-masted schooner *Grana* in 1918, she was re-engined in 1920 when acquired by Everard, but her sailing gear not removed until re-engined again in 1925, renamed *Capable*, to trade as a motor coaster.

In 1986 Charlie Fielder recalled '*Amenity* had a crew of six hands and was, when loaded, very heavy to steer. Fred Bailey had lost two fingers from his right hand and so found it difficult to grip the wheel in bad weather, so I used to help him out. If I did any extra work for him he would always repay me in kind, buying books for me to read. He was a fine coasting seaman and I am proud to have sailed with him. At one time he skippered his own barge, *Gravelines III*. In

addition to working other men's craft he had commanded the X Lighter[1] 'beetle barge' motor tanker *Wander* and the M.V.s *Capable* and *Aseity*.

[1] X-Lighters, nicknamed 'Beetles', were landing craft built for the W.W.I Dardanelles campaign, then converted for commercial carrying.

'I always thought that the tragedy of losing two of his crew in the *Harriot* weighed heavily on him. Once we were passing between Sunderland Piers, bound for Monks Wear Mouth Staithe to load coal for Colchester Gasworks and he spoke to me about it. "Charlie", he said, "You're rather impetuous and it's a bad habit. The place we are passing was the scene of one of the greatest mistakes I've ever made".

'This was where, in 1901, his schooner *Harriot*[2] struck the pierhead in a gale and was lost with only one other survivor.

"It was blowing a gale of wind at the time and visibility was poor. I was trying to keep her up to the weather pierhead and made a miscalculation and we hit the lee pierhead. The sea overwhelmed us and as we struck, the bowsprit mounted the pier, and after a struggle I was able to climb along it and so get ashore." '

The red exercise book concludes with a list of addresses, including that of Mr. K. Munro of S.S. *Tirydail* and others, possibly of accommodation for seamen, in Antwerp, Strood, Goole, Dysart, Caister-on-Sea, Middlesbrough, Margate, Colchester and in Hammersmith and Fulham. This is followed by his list of craft in which he served and a note of the courses taken in M.V. *Amenity* and instructions on the opening and closing of valves for pumping discharge, probably on the tanker *Agility*.

Near the end of the notebook, written in pencil, is an undated entry headed 'Brief Summary of days happening. Proceeded along King Street, Hammersmith passing into Metro Station en route for a greengrocers shop, I purchases some fruit. Crossing over Hammersmith Broadway I myself being in company of Mrs. Ada Owen and daughter, also mother of the same. We then take a bus No.11 on passage to Walham Green...' No more than this is written, but perhaps one may speculate as to the subject matter when aware of his circumstances a year or more later.

Charlie Fielder remained with F.T. Everard & Sons Ltd. and served on the coastal tanker *Prowess* from 1932 to 1937. *Prowess* had been built for the company by George Brown & Co., Greenock and launched on Saturday 7th July 1926. The Chief Officer's Log which had been written up by his predecessor came into Charlie Fielder's possession and records her daily passages from the date of the hand-over by her builders, to Capt J. Brown on 26th August, 1926.

[2] This gale raged for four days in November 1901. 17 vessels foundered and at least 65 men drowned.

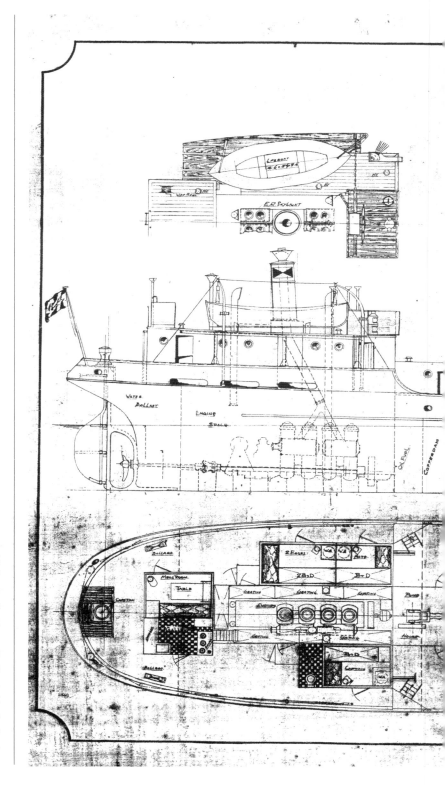

The General Arrangement drawing of the motor tanker *Prowess* as drawn up by her Clydeside builder George Brown & Co, Greenock. Some changes were incorporated before she was finished, the most important being heating coils to her cargo tanks to soften heavy oil and molasses cargoes.

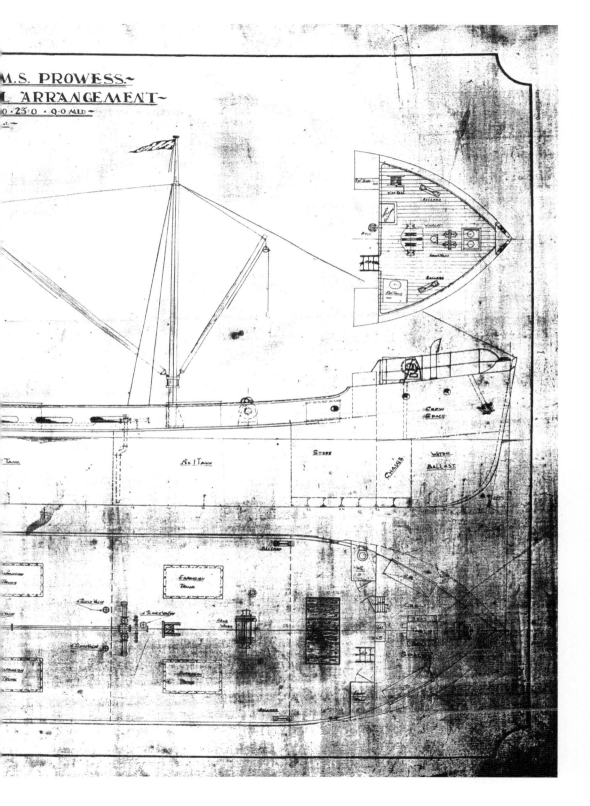

M.S. PROWESS.~
ARRANGEMENT~
0·23·0 · 9·0 MLD~

The new ship left Greenock, on the Clyde, at 8.30 a.m., dropped the Pilot and proceeded at full speed on passage to the Caledonian Canal. The engine had to be stopped at noon when the brake band ran hot, but they were under way again an hour later to carry on around the Mull of Cantyre [sic] and turn due north to pass Lismore Lighthouse into Loch Linnhe at 6.05 a.m. next morning. *Prowess*

Log of the first passage of *Prowess*.

CHIEF OFFICER'S LOG.

Log of the Steam Ship m v *Prowess* Captain *J Brown* 1 Sept 1926

From *Greenock*   Towards *Greenhithe*

HOURS.	COURSE STANDARD COMPASS.	Deviation.	DISTANCE RUN.		WINDS.		Barometer.	REMARKS, &c.
			Knots.	Tnths.	Direction.	Force.		192
1 A.M.	6·0AM		Underway again through to Inverness					
2	9·0AM		Stopped at Inverness for Spare parts of Engine					
3	4·0PM		Underway					
4	5·30PM		Left Sea locks and full Speed on Passage wind E light					
5	10·0PM		~~Kinnaird Head abm~~					
6			2nd Sept 1926					
7	2·40AM		Kinnaird Head Abm 5 miles vis clear · Wind S·E Light					
8	5·0AM		Rattray Head Abm 5 miles vis clear					
9	7·10AM		Buchan Ness Ab 5 miles vis clear Wind S S E light					
10	9·40AM		Girdle Ness " 5 miles " clear					
11	1·30PM		Bell Rock Light ·m° miles vis clear					
12	7·40PM		St Abbs Head abm 5 miles vis clear course S by E					

BEARING AND DISTANCE AT NOON.

TRUE COURSE MADE AT NOON.	DISTANCE.	Latitude by Account.	Latitude Observed.	Tank Soundings.	Longitude by Account.	Longitude by Chronometer.	Variation.	Distance run per Patent Log.	Error per cent. of Patent Log.	Average Sped.

1 P.M.		3rd Sept 1926	
2	12·55AM	Coquet Island ab 5 miles S E by S fine	
3	9·20AM	Whitby abeam Thick fog	
4	1·30PM	Flamburgh Head abeam Clear course S B J E	
5	10·0PM	Outer Dowsing abm close clear	
6			
7		4rd Sept 1926	
8	12·55AM	Cromer Lt abm 5 miles clear	
9	3·0AM	Haisboro Lt " 5 miles clear	
10	4·30AM	Cockle Lt v " close	
11	5·20AM	St Nicolas " close	
12	6·15AM	Newcome Bouy " close clear	

ON THE LOOK OUT.		NAME.		LANTERNS HUNG OUT.	
				FROM	TO
FROM 7·10AM	TO	Orfordness abeam 2 miles		"	"
11·0AM		Gunflut Lt " close		"	"
1·15PM		Sunmiddle Lt v close		"	"
2·0PM		Maplin Lt H close		"	"
2·40PM		Mouse Lt v "		"	"
3·30PM		None Lt v "		"	"
8·0PM		" Arrived Greenhithe moored Globe Bouy		Chief	

Master.   Chief

"GLASGOW" PATTERN No. 2.

reached Corpach Sea Lock at 10.15 a.m. and carried on through the Canal. At 2 p.m. they had more engine trouble at Benavie and stopped until 7.30 a.m. next morning. They were under way for just an hour and half when they had to stop at Gairlochy where the crew rigged up tackle for lifting, perhaps to remove and repair an engine part. They lay there for a couple of days until at noon on 31st

The western entrance to the Caledonian Canal at Corpach, in the shadow of Ben Nevis, a very different backdrop to the flatland of East Anglia and The Netherlands, where *Prowess* mainly plied her trade.

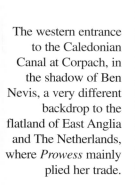

August, any problem resolved, they got under way again through Loch Lochy. By 9.40 p.m. it was getting too dark to continue so they stopped for the night. Under way at 6.00 a.m. next morning *Prowess* reached Inverness at 9.00 a.m. where they picked up spares for the engine, no doubt needed to address the earlier problems. It was not until 4.00 that afternoon that they were able to get under way again, clearing the sea lock at 5.30 p.m. to resume full speed in a light south-east wind with a change of course S by E at St. Abbs Head at 7.40 p.m. Flamborough Head was abeam at 1.30 p.m. on 3rd September, Cromer light at 12.55 on 4th, Orfordness at 9.10 a.m., Swin Middle 1.15 p.m.; the Nore light at 3.30 p.m., arriving at Greenhithe to moor on the Globe Buoy at 8.00 p.m. on 4th September.

Capt. Brown handed over to his colleague, the designated master Capt. Coker, to start her first passage to Rouen at 12.30 on 5th September passing Cap D'Antifer at 11.15 a.m. next morning and anchoring in Le Havre Roads at 12.10. They were berthed at the jetty ready for loading Benzol[3] at 6.45 p.m., finished loading just before midnight on 7th September, to be ready to leave at 6.00 a.m. next morning. Capt Coker's engineer had trouble with the blow-lamp starters which held up departure for an hour but they then had a clear run overnight for 56 hours

[3.] Benzol, a crude form of benzene obtained from coal gas or tar and used as fuel.

Keadby Jetty,
Everard's *Cambria*,
Goldsmith's *Scotia*
beyond, a destination
served by the
sailormen and
motor-ships of both
companies.

to anchor off Hull to await clearance. *Prowess* completed her maiden voyage in trade at Keadby Jetty, up the River Trent, at 10.30 on 12th September,1926.

After unloading she sailed from Keadby to Rouen on the River Seine to load for Coryton, Thames Haven. Then followed further passages to Lymington where, on one occasion, Capt. Coker rang up the London office to report trouble with the main engine and was asked to hang on for an engineer from Plenty & Co., the engine's maker from Newbury, just 56 miles away.

Repairs accomplished, a passage to Antwerp for a cargo was delayed due to thick fog; on arrival it was Sunday 3rd October so no work was done in the Belgian port. Next day was spent cleaning the ship and painting before the return to Thames Haven where the pump would not suck up the cargo. However, by 9th October discharging was completed and, towing a lighter from Shell Haven, *Prowess* ran into a gale of wind in the Lower Hope which caused all the tow ropes to part. The lighter ran into the ship denting her hull but was secured again and they berthed at Greenhithe to await orders. For the next three days she remained at the firm's yard, then went back to work. The Logbook continues to record the detail of each passage until 20th February 1928, all written in a neat hand which could be that of Capt. Coker himself.

After initial problems with her machinery, *Prowess* was to become a long-serving, though not always reliable, member of the Everard fleet.

Following the death of the founder of F.T. Everard & Sons Ltd. in 1929, his son, Fred. W. became Chairman, and with his brothers and sister continued to expand the dry cargo and tanker fleets. The barge yard in the Greenhithe High Street was already part of a thriving river community lying off the old road from Dartford to Gravesend and between the Swanscombe and Stone Marshes. From the river the village lay directly opposite Stone Ness at the end of St. Clement's or Fiddler's Reach and Long Reach. A contemporary Port Guide Map published by Imray, Laurie, Norie & Wilson shows The Empire Paper Mills, built in the grounds of Ingress Park, with the Training Ship *Worcester* lying off the Kentish shore with Crouch, the barge builders just down stream of Greenhithe Causeway, the Pier Hotel and Tester Brothers Ltd., the tug and lightermen. Then Everard's office and wharf is shown with the White Hart causeway just upstream and the White Hart Hotel all to the north of the High Street, followed by Globe Pier, Arethusa Wharf and the various jetties of the Cement Works and rail link.

On the Essex side of the river, the open West Thurrock Marshes were interrupted by the Tunnel Cement Works, their tramway and jetty within which was an anchorage and Everard's barge roads buoy. Upstream, after Thurrock Chalk & Whiting Co. Ltd. was Jurgens Wharf where, after 1921, many well known brands of

The Tunnel Cement works, once the largest in western europe, were connected to the company's wharf by a tramway. The tank locomotives 'Anglo-Dane' and 'Tunnel' and many more besides, pulled wagons of raw materials and finished product to and from the Thurrock plant.

margarine were produced. Continuing upstream were Purfleet Wharf & Saw Mills Ltd. and Caspian Wharf with two buoys off and tanks ashore. This was where Everard craft went to refuel at the Anglo-American Oil Co. pier. Anglo also had terminals at Hull and elsewhere and the Everard tankers regularly transported a variety of oils between them. The company had begun life in 1888 and was the first foreign affiliate of John D. Rockefeller's U.S. company, the Standard Oil Trust. It had a head office at Bishopsgate, London and the depot at Purfleet which stored paraffin shipped from New York for use in lamps throughout England. In 1911, the U.S. Supreme Court ordered the dissolution of the Standard Oil Trust resulting in the spin-off of 33 companies, one of which, Standard Oil (New Jersey) acquired Anglo. The British affiliate remained with the New Jersey company and in 1934, it took a phonetic version of the initials of Standard Oil (SO = Esso) as one of its brand names, still familiar today. In 1951, Esso was adopted as the company name in the U.K.

46

Looking down river, in the foreground, the Anglo American Oil jetty; beyond was Caspian Wharf; then a ship alongside Purfleet Wharf & Saw Mills jetty; next the B.P. jetty; then Jurgens Wharf; next the piers of Thurrock Chalk and Whiting Co.; in the distance, Tunnel Cement Wharf.

Everard forged long term trading links with Anglo and a number of multinational organisations, particularly Van den Berghs Ltd., later part of Unilever plc, carrying much of their raw materials between the two arms of the company in The Netherlands and the U.K. There were many other wharves served by the Everard ships including those at Erith, East Greenwich, Millwall, Rotherhithe and even as far upstream as Hammersmith, where the Distillers Company had a wharf.

The Fielder family played their part in these trades and the red exercise book in which Charles recorded his voyages was to be superseded by the 'Scrap Logbooks' maintained by the deck officers of the motor tanker *Prowess* for the years 1933 - 1937 which form the basis for most of the following chapters. Her voyages were all within the home-trade limits from Ushant, off the Brittany coast of France, near Brest in the south-west, to the River Elbe which served Hamburg in the north-east. It was not necessary for the masters and mates of ships trading coastwise within these limited to be accredited under the Merchant Shipping Acts and many owners took advantage of this rule to engage crews without

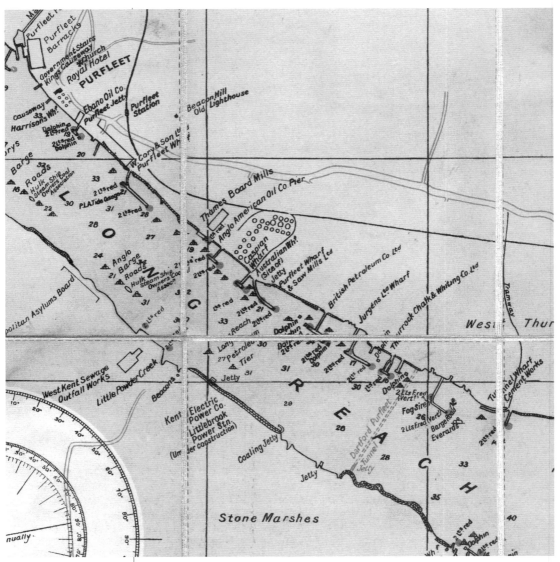

Part of a 1937 River Thames Wharf Chart by Imray, Laurie, Norie & Wilson Ltd., which illustrates the Purfleet and Thurrock jetties, just upriver from the Everard yard at Greenhithe on the south side of the Thames.

such qualifications; relying on years of experience, many of which Charlie Fielder had acquired.

Fielder acquired a copy of The Pilot's Guide for the English Channel. The book was well used with much thumbed pages for the Downs and south coast into which he tucked, apparently as a page marker, the invoice from Revel Brothers for 8 bags of Galley Coal dated 16 Sept. 1937, and a report that medals for seamen for the 1914-18 war were being issued. Another book was the Guide to the Northsea-Canal and the Harbours of Ijmuiden & Amsterdam for 1936, published and sold in Amsterdam. It was written in English with the official translation of the General Regulations and Special Rules for the Pilotage Service in the Kingdom of The Netherlands by Royal Decree of January 22nd 1902, Harbour Dues, tables of distances, and much else including Charts of the Harbours. The need for this book is quite apparent from the pattern of trade which Charlie Fielder was to follow during the ensuing years.

During the years after *Prowess* joined the Everard fleet, but before Charlie had joined her, personal tragedy would strike at the Fielder family flat, 110, Riverside Gardens, Hammersmith. Becky had contracted Tuberculosis. Husband Charlie was by her side when she died on 29th April 1931, aged 56. Her youngest son recalls that "I and my brother Gordon, who was a van boy for a company named Palmers Store in King Street, Hammersmith, were looked after by our wonderful sister Emily, who saw to it that we behaved ourselves! At this time we were visited by some clergy who said that as I did not have a mother, I was an orphan, and would be better off in Australia. We contacted dad who knew some friends who got me freed from school early and got me the mate's job on the *Agnes Mary*, which must have been hard for my wonderful dad."

On 8th February 1932, at Flat 73, Thomas Frederick Owen died aged just 28. He was buried in the Hammersmith New Cemetery near Mortlake (entry No.5290) leaving his wife Ada alone in their flat, a widow at 26, with two young children to support.

Happier days at the Riverside Gardens flats, celebrating the Jubilee of King George V and Queen Mary on 6th May 1935.

Charles Henry Fielder joined Everard's *Prowess* on 15th October 1932 in London on a voyage to King's Lynn then to Bergen op Zoom in Holland. The ship then returned to Cantley, near Yarmouth, Norfolk and undertook ten such return voyages during the rest of the year. The ship was taking on a cargo of semi-liquid molasses from the sugar beet processing factory at Cantley for delivery to the Zuid-Nederlandsche Melasse-Spritusfabriek, which by the end of the decade had become Nedalco, returning across the channel in ballast as she did many times in the years to come. Only the bare facts of the voyages were given on the fly sheet of a foolscap size Boots Scribbling Diary for 1933 but from Sunday 1st January 1933 a series of diaries record the daily activities of the ship.

As with, for example, the ferryman's working life, spent crossing and re-crossing the same stretch of water, there was much that was to become routine in the trading pattern of the *Prowess*. This regularity of trade was good for the owner's business and the regular employment of the vessel's crew, though in its baldest data, dates and timings, some of the inevitable monotony involved may touch these pages. To keep faith with that life afloat in the coastal and near continental trades, very few voyages are skipped in this narrative, for to have done so would have betrayed the authenticity of Charlie's story. It must also be recognised that even the ferryman's everyday was different, weather and tide never quite the same. Add to those variants the vagueries of the vessel herself, the man-made frailty of machinery, pumps, engines, etc., and it is easy to envisage the variety that this routine can encompass.

The Cantley sugar factory had been built in 1912 and was the first successful British beet sugar factory, after previous premises at Maldon, Essex (1832) and Lavenham, Suffolk (18 69) had both failed. Under the Anglo-Dutch banner were the six factories built by Joanness Van Rossum: Cantley, Norfolk; Ely, Cambridgeshire; Ipswich, Suffolk; Colwick in Nottingham (1924) and Kelham at Newark, Nottinghamshire (1921); and King's Lynn, Norfolk. The permanent workforce at Cantley was

The Cantley sugar beet processing factory, served by the River Yare. A laden wherry is alongside with more beet to add to the heap already unloaded as the 'campaign' proceeds around the clock.

over a hundred rising during the processing 'campaign' which lasted about four months during which period it operated around the clock. The factory had been built about fifteen miles from the head of navigation at Norwich, about half way along the River Yare to the North Sea. Some three miles downstream is Reedham Ferry, the marshes, the new cut to St. Olaves on the River Waveney and the railway swing bridge. Then the river widens for about four miles through Breydon Water, below which, 28.7 miles from Norwich, is the Great Yarmouth Haven Bascule Bridge. Some three miles further downstream lies Gorleston and the mouth of the river, the piers and the North Sea. To the north lay Yarmouth Roads, sheltered by the Scroby Sands; to the south, Corton Roads and the sands.

Sailing wherries delivered the beet harvest for processing until sail gave way to power, motorised ex. sailing wherries, towing de-rigged wherries deep laden with beet for Cantley.

51

Breydon Swing Bridge carried the railway across the River Yare by Breydon Water. Built in 1903, it was to operate for just 50 years, closing in 1953, demolished 10 years later.

Sunday 1st January, 1933 saw *Prowess* lying at the Cantley sugar beet factory. She was engaged in lightening S.S. *Alchymist* for refloating, then tending her towage and providing general assistance on the passage down river to Yarmouth. *Alchymist* was a 382 ton steam tanker, 147.5 ft. in length, with a beam of 24.1 ft. and depth of 12.8 ft. and was owned by Everard until 1950. She had been bought in March, 1922 from Thomas Burt Haywood, of London having been built to carry wood tar for the firm of timber merchants. The steam heating coils in her cargo tanks were the result of fifty years of testing and experience by her first owners. She had been cleaned up by Everards who found that the technology was transferable to the carriage of edible oils in bulk.

The trade was instantly revolutionised by eliminating the need for barrels and all the associated handling costs and leakages. She proved very successful and over the next few years further tankers were ordered, their design based on the experience gained. Although somewhat smaller, to enable her to work to and from inland wharves, *Prowess* had the same system of heating coils to facilitate the carriage of molasses in each of her tanks. It seems that the Company may have decided that this was to be the last attempt to load molasses directly into *Alchymist* at Cantley.

Monday morning saw *Prowess* lying alongside at Wenn's Wharf, Gt. Yarmouth, awaiting daylight to leave at 9.40 a.m.

The *Alchymist*, had already seen 26 years service for her first owners before she joined Everard, but was to do 28 more before being scrapped at Grays in 1950. Although steam power was already being superceded, its availability for the heating coils to soften the cargo for pumping extended the service life of such craft.

to return to the factory. She moored at 12.30 after a slight delay owing to high winds which set her across the river from where she had to be hove off from the opposite bank. At 2.10 p.m. she commenced loading molasses with the crew attending the valves to trim the ship. They finished loading at 7 p.m., stopped the valves and pumping to record the ships draught as 7' 8" forward, 8' 6" aft. One ton of coals and fresh water were taken onboard whilst there.

On Tuesday morning the pipe line was disconnected but their departure was delayed due to an abnormally bad tide and weather conditions. At 12.30 a.m. they left Cantley for Yarmouth, however strong under currents seemed to make the ship quite unmanageable at times, once causing her to strike the bank of the river. She passed through Breydon Swing Bridge at 2.20 p.m. to arrive at Wenn's Wharf, Gt. Yarmouth and moor to the south west quay an hour later. After a couple of hours the skipper received reports of bad weather conditions outside the harbour and decided to stop there to await a more favourable outlook before crossing the channel to Bergen op Zoom.

The crew spent the time engaged in a variety of tasks, including trimming the coal away for safety; (the log is always concerned to show that the crew were fully and productively active!), but at 11.45, slack water, on 4th January, the skipper decided to proceed to sea. After an hour they were abeam Corton Light and the log was streamed. The weather was overcast with bright intervals and a fresh south-west wind, the sea was choppy as they steered a compass course south-east by south. Off the Gabbard at 5.00, late afternoon, the wind was increasing and the ship rolling and pitching about and shipping seas aboard. *Prowess* laboured on to sight Wescapelle Light at midnight, altered course for the Steen Bank buoy and at 2.45 a.m., with the Veerse Gat buoy abeam they were relieved to find smoother water. They then had to cruise about in dull and cloudy weather awaiting a Pilot and customs clearance.

The Dutch officials came aboard at 6.30 a.m., the tanks were inspected, sealed and the Customs' men departed. With the Pilot in charge *Prowess* left Zierikzee at 6.50 to arrived at the

Looking down the Bergen op Zoom creek, the tide gone and all vessels hard aground. To the left is the quay and storage tanks of the Nedalco Spiritusfabriek, *Prowess*'s destination.

entrance to Bergen op Zoom creek at 09.40 a.m.. Five minutes later they were aground with the tide ebbing! They had to wait until at 8.30 p.m. the ship floated on the rising tide and at 9.15 p.m. she made the second berth at the Spiritusfabriek Berth, Bergen op Zoom with the wind blowing hard and raining in squalls.

Bergen op Zoom was a fishing port of North Brabant, S.W. Netherlands, at the junction of East Schelde and the Zoom Rivers, with a local economy dependent on the sugar industry and the importation of the Norfolk beet harvest.

Next morning they waited for Customs to unseal the tanks and dip them for measurement. The crew busied themselves with general ship's work; the brass in the wheelhouse needed cleaning and the steam pipes for Nos. 3 and 4 tank coils had to be connected. It was 3 p.m. (Dutch time) before Customs unsealed the tanks and the shore pumpman turned on the steam to send it through the coils to heat and thin the molasses for the cargo to be pumped out. It took until 9.30 p.m. before the ship was hove alongside, moored and the land pipelines connected to commence discharging. An hour later the small deck engine pump was put in gear, but it was a further 45 minutes before the molasses was warm enough to flow without crystallising in the delivery pipes.

The crew were keeping watch until 3 a.m. next morning, which greeted them wet and squally, before abating and becoming fine with bright intervals. The log for Saturday 7th January records that at 3.45 a.m. they had finished pumping the cargo and the pump stopped to await shore cleaners from the factory to come aboard to clear the tanks of any residual molasses. The Pilot came aboard at 8.30 a.m. to await the tide to float the ship, while the crew disconnected the steam pipes from the coils. At 10.10 a.m. the engine was started and *Prowess* got under way for England. Arriving off Zierikzee at 12.45 they waited customs clearance, dropped the Pilot and ballasted the ship with overboard water, before they were on passage back for the next cargo.

On Sunday morning at 3.15 a.m. *Prowess* berthed at Gt. Yarmouth and, it would seem, the master and crew turned in for a nap (but such things are not mentioned in the log). By 7.15 they were up and pumping out the ballast water, then starting the ship's engine to return to Cantley, but on arrival at the factory they were ordered to go back to assist S.S.*Tartary* which they had left berthed alongside in Gt. Yarmouth. She was another steam tanker owned by the firm which, in 1938, was destined to be destroyed by an explosion after grounding off Happisburgh, Norfolk, while on passage from Zaandam to Hull with a cargo of linseed oil.

S.S. *Tartary*, like
Alchymist, was an ex.
Burt, Boulton &
Haywood tar carrier,
unlike *Alchymist* she
was to be short-lived,
lost as a result of an
explosion when less
than 15 years old.

Back at Yarmouth *Tartary* failed to float and *Prowess* had to await the next flood tide. It seems they were successful at the second attempt as the next entry in the diary made after their arrival back at the factory jetty is of the shore gang coupling up the pipes for the next load of molasses. While tending the valves for trimming the ship, the crew were engaged in painting, cutting in the white band around the hull. The cargo was intended to be transferred to S.S. *Alchymist*, but they had to await the morning tide for a daylight passage down the River Wensum. Arriving at Gt. Yarmouth quay at 4 p.m. they discovered that the *Alchymist* had not arrived from London. It was not until 6.00 a.m. on Thursday that she had berthed. The crew warped *Prowess* alongside to start the transshipment. The larger tanker was able to supply the steam to the coils to warm the molasses to enable the cargo to be pumped over. The rest of the day the crew of the *Prowess* made fenders while the mate superintended the pumping operation.

On Friday 13th January *Prowess* was back at Cantley to load while the crew painted her name and Port of Registry on the transom rail. This time the load was for Holland with an uneventful crossing under an overcast sky with light variable winds. At Bergen op Zoom the tank coils were supplied with steam, but pumping had to be suspended as the thread of the bolts of the clutch gear in the pump-house were stripped. The engineer took some three hours to carry out a repair before unloading could start. The engine was started in time to let go the ship at 7.50 on Thursday 19th to proceed on passage for Cantley, but after customs clearance at Zierikzee piers at 10.25 a.m. the skipper decided to go into the Veerse Gat anchorage owing to thick fog. *Prowess* remained at anchor in dense fog all day and all night. In much improved conditions in the morning, with a light breeze, the ship left the Veerse Gat anchorage at 7 a.m. in moderate visibility. The crew started pumping the ballast water out of the tanks to enter Gt. Yarmouth at 8 p.m. that evening.

After loading, delivering and discharging the next cargo, the *Prowess* was ordered back to Gravesend to have the regulation Plimsoll marks painted on the ship's sides, and rigging gangways and deck life-saving apparatus. There was a change in cargo; in place of molasses *Prowess* was sent to Purfleet to load mineral oils. On Monday 30th January 1933 she left Greenhithe for Hull laden

The Hull River and Old Harbour join the River Humber, bottom right, amidst wharves and industry, various craft almost blocking the waterway. Most of *Prowess's* calls were further up-river, beyond the prominent Clarence Mills, top centre.

[1] Red oil is a form of palm oil used in cooking and nuclear reactors!
[2] Seaton's, founded in 1840 by John Love Seaton, one-time Mayor of Hull, is still in the vegetable oil business, relocating from Hull to nearby Hessle in 2003.

with spindle oil in No.3 tank and red oil[1] in tanks 1, 2, and 4. They unloaded at the Anglo American Oil Co. wharf in the River Hull at 10 p.m. on Wednesday 1st February and next morning the ship was towed stern first with her anchor down on the flood tide up to Seaton's Wharf[2] to discharge 150 tons of the red lubricating oil to finish discharging at 3 p.m. on Friday 3rd February.

The next cargo was to be molasses again so the crew were set to cleaning the tanks to await the 11 p.m. tide, but the main engine had a problem with the air valves and refused to start. Ballast water was pumped into tanks 1 and 2 but the engine still would not start so the Pilot left. On Saturday morning at 2 a.m., with the ship's engine still refusing to start, engineers came and eventually succeeded in getting the engine running for a short trial. It was by then too late for the tide so it was not until 12.30 that the ship could get away down the River Hull in charge of a Pilot who was put ashore before *Prowess* was underway for Gt. Yarmouth.

She arrived at 3 a.m. on Sunday 5th to wait for the bridge to open and take the sailing barge *Alf Everard* in tow to Cantley to prepare for loading and an approaching gale. The shore men

The *Alf Everard* under tow, loaded for sea, in company with a square sailed Humber keel and others astern. The photograph is of the River Trent, the barge having loaded coal at Keadby wharf.

arrived at 7.30 next morning to connect pipes with the mate left tending the loading. The following afternoon the *Alf Everard* was towed back to Gt. Yarmouth where the master of the *Prowess* decided that owing to weather conditions it was better to wait before leaving Yarmouth on passage for Bergen op Zoom. They left on Wednesday 8th but at midday ran into thick fog and rain squalls. Seven hours later they sighted a buoy which when approached proved to be the East Gat light buoy, an hour later they reached the Veerse Gat anchorage and let go 20 fathoms of chain to await daylight and the passage to Zierikzee for clearance. Discharging was completed on Friday 10th to start the passage back to England. The next cargo was loaded on 13th February to cross to Holland and unload on 16th.

The following freight was to be loaded at Colchester, Essex so *Prowess* sailed from Bergen at 8.30 a.m. on Saturday 18th February to the Rolling Grounds off Harwich. They found little water in the River Colne before swinging ready to moor at the Gas Works Wharf on Monday morning. The crew were ready next morning but there was insufficient water so they were set to wipe the tanks and red lead paint below the water line. The Quay Master directed the attempt to come alongside on the evening tide but they had to wait

OWEN PARRY.
COLCHESTER OIL MILLS

OWEN PARRY LTS. OIL MILLS, COLCHESTER

Owen Parry's oil mill at Colchester Hythe, from a battered postcard of 1905, but little changed in the following 50 years. *Prowess* arrived stern first having swung off the Gas Works Wharf.

until the following morning before they were able to pull her close to the quay and the dock sheds to take on fresh water. They reached Owen Parry's Wharf at New Hythe Quay, Colchester, to moor at 8.30 a.m. on 21st February to load 208 tons of linseed oil. The crew finished the remaining painting of the bulwarks while awaiting the tide on Thursday 23rd. At 11.15 a.m. the main engine was ordered, the boat was lifted aboard and stowed above the pump room and the ship left down the Colne with a Pilot on board. He left in his small boat an hour later whilst *Prowess* proceeded for Erith. Fog in the Lower Rands called for reduced speed, before berthing at the Erith Oil Works Jetty to await further orders.

On Friday morning they were ordered to the inside jetty berth to discharge the oil. The expected passage to Cantley for Rotterdam was cancelled and they lay alongside the firm's *Asperity* at Greenhithe awaiting orders, the crew getting aboard some towing hawsers and rope.

Orders arrived at 2 p.m. on Monday 27th February to proceed to Cantley to load molasses for Bergen op Zoom again. Adverse weather delayed the return to Greenhithe on 8th March for repairs including the replacement of the propeller. While this work was undertaken the mate was ordered to Faversham as lighterman to take a newly launched barge in tow from Faversham to Greenhithe. On Friday the new bronze propeller was fitted so that at midday on Saturday 11th March *Prowess* left for trials for an hour, before proceeding on passage for Selby, Yorkshire.

Orfordness was sighted abeam just after midnight; Cromer at 4.35 a.m.; Spurn light was abeam just after midday, then came the run up the Humber past Hull, Trent Falls and Blacktoft Jetty to arrive at Goole at 6 pm. There they waited for an hour and a half to leave just sufficient time to arrive on the tide at Selby at 9.45 p.m. on Sunday evening. On the morning of Monday 13th the ship was shifted to the second outer berth to be ready for loading. The crew were left splicing and rigging new light halliards, chipping and painting the deck ventilators and funnel badges. At 1.15 p.m. loading of 215 tons of P.K. oil[3] was started and was to finish six hours later when the tank tops were screwed tightly down. After a slight delay *Prowess* got away to pass through Selby Railway Bridges to moor alongside the Railway Quay for the night. With the Pilot in charge they were under way down the Ouse at 6.10 a.m. He was dropped off at the New Holland light-float and they were away out of the Humber on passage to London.

No berth was available when they arrived alongside the Jurgens Jetty, Purfleet, at 2 p.m. on Wednesday 15th so they shifted to lie alongside the firms tanker, S.S. *Tartary* at a lower berth. Her steam pipes were connected to the steam coils on *Prowess* and a shore pump finished discharging the oil while the crew were engaged in scraping tank bottoms and were still working on Friday when the ship returned to Greenhithe to await orders. At

[3.] PK is an abbreviation for either Palm kernel or Peanut kernel oil. Palm kernel oil is used in the manufacture of soap (e.g. Palmolive), whilst Peanut kernel oil is used for foodstuffs. As the consignee was Jurgens, the margarine makers, it would be the latter.

midday *Prowess* picked up the big ship mooring buoy to be in attendance with the new M.V. *Actuality* which was towed to Greenhithe to have her engine installed, and for bunkering oil from the tug/tender *Co-operator*. Once taking bunkers was completed, *Co-operator* and *Prowess* moved to another mooring close by, *Prowess* still awaiting orders.

Everard's tug/tender *Co-operator* was built for Lincoln Equitable Co-operative Industrial Society in 1913.

On Monday it was blowing a gale of wind and Charlie Fielder was marooned ashore, but he got on board at 11 a.m. when an able seaman was ordered on to the tug/tender *Stonebow* to sort out the excessive jumping of the mooring buoy. The roads wire had broken, so another head wire had to be put out, but the weather was fining down. At last, at noon on 20th March 1933, the Captain received orders to report to Customs for clearance and move to Thamesdown Oil Refineries to load 150 ton of fuel oil for Jersey, Channel Isles. So at 8.00 a.m. she went alongside the oil jetties, the tanks were filled, dipped and sampled and Prowess proceeded on passage at 11.30 a.m. passing the Girdler Light at 2.00 p.m.; South Foreland 6 p.m.; Dungeness 9.15 p.m.; Beachy Head 1.15 a.m. Wednesday morning;

The firm's *Stonebow* was also built in 1913, for the East Anglian Navigation Co. of Sleaford, joining Everard in 1919.

Owers Bank Light vessel was reached at 6.25 a.m. but by 11 a.m., when 30 miles from the Owers, *Prowess* had to turn back due to a strong southerly wind and increasing sea. By 3.20 p.m. they were alongside the firm's motor vessel *Grit* to wait for the first of the ebb and at 9 a.m. they let go to proceed to a safe anchorage off Lymington at 'Jack in the Basket' Roads with 25 fathoms out and weather-bound. They remained there sheltering in the strong south-easterly wind until 5.45 p.m. when the Captain decided to weigh anchor to go over to Yarmouth, Isle of Wight and land a small boat ashore for stores and provisions.

It was still blowing next day, but on Saturday they were underway at 1.35 a.m. to resume the passage for Jersey, logging 67 miles to Cape la Hague. A Pilot was picked up at 3.20 p.m. to enter St. Helier Harbour, where there was sufficient water by 4.50 to pass through the piers and wait alongside the quay for water at the Jersey Power Station berth, where *Prowess* moored at 5.10 p.m.

Pump out of the fuel oil cargo was intermittently delayed by problems with the suction valves which led to stoppages. Discharging was finished at 1.30 p.m. on Sunday 26th March and the ship sailed in charge of the Pilot five hours later. Once he had left they proceeded at full speed for London in light variable winds: Beachy Head 3 a.m.; South Foreland 10.20 a.m.; Southend Pier abeam at 3 p.m.; to arrive at Greenhithe buoys at 7.10 p.m. and receive orders to wash out the tanks in the morning. This involved moving alongside the *Co-operator* to empty the remnants of the fuel oil, then leaving the Lower Roads to go alongside the steaming barge at the Coal Wharf for water to fill the tanks for cleaning, before returning to the Roads while the crew washed and wiped out the *Prowess's* tanks.

On the morning of Wednesday 29th March, *Prowess* moved to the Anglo American Wharf, Purfleet, to load lubricating oil for Hull, in all around 200 tons, including 50 tons of red oil. She left the wharf 4.45 p.m. in fine weather and a moderate southerly wind and anchored in White Booth Roads in the River Humber, with 20 fathoms out to await the morning tide. She arrived at Anglo American's Hull wharf to discharge part of the cargo at 8 a.m., 50 tons of red lubricating oil from tank No.3. Finished at 2.30 p.m., *Prowess* got under way with a tug and Pilot in attendance to proceed to Seaton's Wharf in the Old Harbour. On

Saturday 1st April shore pipelines were connected for the shoremen to start the discharge of the remaining 150 tons while the crew chipped the starboard bulwarks and painted them with red lead to keep the rust at bay.

Sunday was a day of rest, leaving the remainder of the cargo to be discharged on Monday morning. Then the crew were engaged in cleaning tanks for the next cargo while the ship proceeded on passage up river to Selby at 9.30 p.m., picking up the Goole Pilot, who was dropped at Goole Pier at 12.25 next morning, when the Selby Pilot came aboard. He took them to their loading berth, the Olympia Mills, to take on 100 tons of cotton seed oil and 100 tons of ground nut oil. Loading was finished at 10.35 a.m. and *Prowess* left at 11.45 for Goole in charge of the local Pilot but, as there was insufficient water to carry on down river, they anchored to await the next tide. Just after midnight they left Goole Piers in the charge of a Pilot, bound for London, via Hull, where the Pilot disembarked into a cutter and *Prowess* carried on up the east coast past Orfordness, where a fuel pipe burst causing the ship to stop for 20 minutes.

The vast Olympia Mills complex at Selby on the River Ouse.

They continued through the night but ran into thick fog and were forced to anchor off Leigh, in the Thames Estuary, at 5.30 a.m. By 8.55 the fog had lifted a bit and they were under way

to anchor off Jurgens Wharf, Purfleet, to await orders to go alongside. After discharging some of the ground nut oil into wagons, taking about 22 minutes to load each of them, the rest was discharged ashore so that the ship could leave the wharf at just after 9.00 that evening for Silvertown, to the John Knights Soap Works, where next morning the cotton oil was discharged. At 6 p.m. the crew finished wiping out the tanks and received orders for Coryton, waiting until the tide turned at 11.30 for the passage down river.

John Knights Soap Works at Silvertown opened in 1880, having moved from Wapping where it was founded in 1817. It is now part of the Unilever corporation.

Prowess moored alongside at 8.50 a.m. to start to load fuel oil for Newhaven, Sussex, taking on 227 tons giving the ship a draught of 8'0" forward, 9'6" aft. Leaving at one o'clock she entered Newhaven in thick fog at 4 a.m. B.S.T. to await the tide to moor alongside the East Quay. They had to wait until 8.45 to proceed over to the discharging berth on the Southern Railway Oil Jetty. The oil was pumped overside into *Nitrogen*, a tank barge, while the crew painted the starboard bulwark a buff colour. At 3.30 p.m. the discharge was completed, and orders had been received to return to Coryton. *Prowess* left Newhaven to run into thick fog off Beachy Head, but was back at Coryton at 11.30 a.m. on Tuesday 11th April after spending six hours at anchor in the Gore Channel awaiting daylight.

A further 227 tons of fuel was loaded for Newhaven, returning on Thursday 13th to load yet another, but as it was

Easter *Prowess* returned to Greenhithe for bunkering. On Good Friday S.S. *Aridity* and on Saturday *Acclivity* arrived for stores. The log states that no work was done on Easter

Sunday. Monday was a Bank Holiday but *Prowess* sailed for Newhaven to discharge next day and return for a further 220 tons of fuel oil on Wednesday 19th. She returned to the Greenhithe repair yard on 23rd April to be ordered off afloat on Wednesday 26th to lay alongside S.S. *Alchymist*.

The next voyage was to Newcastle, leaving on Friday 28th April and returning to Purfleet on 4th May to load spindle oil for the Victoria Dock, not London, but Dundee, Scotland, which was delivered there four days later. She had the surprise and good fortune of a return cargo of lubricating oil which was discharged to the firm's barges *Compass* and *Cowl* at Greenhithe on the morning of Monday 15th May, *Prowess* having arrived 'home' on the Friday prior to the weekend, the balance of the cargo discharged at the Thames Haven Oil Jetty.

It was time for *Prowess* to return to the molasses trade, but instead of loading at Cantley the ship was ordered to load at King's Lynn, another of the six sugar factories built by Johannes Van Rossum. The crew were set to wash out the tanks with the plan to leave Greenhithe at 3 p.m. on Tuesday 16th May. With the wind freshening, they took on water ballast off Orfordness at midnight, passing Cromer eight hours later and picking up the Lynn Pilot at

The King's Lynn sugar beet processing plant with its jetty fronting the River Great Ouse.

the Bar Buoy at 12.50. They arrived at Lynn Dock wall at 2.05 p.m. and whilst waiting at Boal Quay for the tide to ebb, to give sufficient headroom under the low bridge, the crew unshipped the mast, derricks and funnel. She was able to leave the Dock pier at 4.30 p.m., clear the bridge and arrive alongside the King's Lynn Beet Sugar Factory at 5.15 to be ready for shore men to connect their pipe lines at 7.30 next morning. Rather slow progress was made with loading owing to shore pump machinery trouble and they finished for the day at 4.45 p.m.

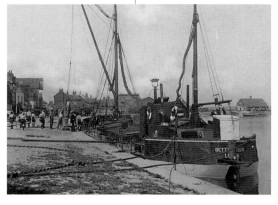

The motor vessel *Betty Hudson*, seen here at Wells-next-the-Sea, like *Prowess*, set sails when the wind served.

Prowess had to move next day to let a coal barge into the berth but the sugar refinery finished loading her at 2 p.m. and the Customs officials dipped and sealed the tanks an hour and a half later. The Pilot was on board at 5.30 to wait about 20 minutes for sufficient air draft under the bridges and they moored at buoys alongside M.V. *Betty Hudson* to await the morning tide.

The low bridge that restricted access to the King's Lynn sugar factory carried track that was redundant before the Beeching axe. It was demolished in 1959.

Some forty years later, in 1977, Charlie Fielder wrote to East Coast Digest about the King's Lynn sugar trade. 'We did mostly cargoes of beet molasses away from the factory to a place called Bergen op Zoom on the East Schelde, calling at Zierikzee for Customs. Pilotage to and from Lynn was compulsory. *Prowess* was rather high for the bridge and we waited at the buoys for clearance. The procedure for negotiating the bridge at Boal Quay was to watch out for special marks and when these were uncovered, we could proceed to the bridge, place our ship's head tight under the upper side of it and reeve a slip wire over one of the girders to hold her there. I would then keep watch and when I could see a chink of daylight over the wheelhouse I'd signal to the skipper, who was standing at the wheel. We would then let go the wire, let the ship drop astern for a few yards, then come full ahead on the engine. The effect of this was for the propeller to drag the stern down about eight inches, which gave us just enough room to get under the bridge. When we got to the jetty the ship's head would be placed to it, and a head wire got round a pile, for her then to come slow ahead with the helm to starboard and sheer the stern to, by the aid of a back spring. This took place on the ebb-tide, so we were almost on the ground by then. When coming away, loaded, we left as soon as we floated, swung and then full ahead at the bridge, just saving our height under it on the flood tide.' It sounds like it was a perilous and risky exercise.

The Pilot was on board at 3.50 a.m. on Saturday 20th May 1933, to proceed on passage for Ipswich. He was dropped at 5.10 and *Prowess* anchored below Pin Mill village at 10.25 p.m. to await daylight, with 15 fathoms of chain out. They were under way at 4.55 a.m. and arrived at Ipswich quay to moor before shifting off into the Dock where the grain ship *Archibald Russell* was occupying some of their berth. Gustaf Erikson's 270 foot long, 2148 ton four masted barque *Archibald Russell* had sailed from Wallaroo to Falmouth with a cargo of wheat in 119 days. At 11.30 *Prowess* moved further down the quay into a berth ready to discharge next day. At 8 a.m. the steaming barge came alongside to connect their pipelines, a Customs official broke the seals, dipped the tanks and then the steam was sent through the heating coils in the cargo tanks so that the 215 tons of molasses could be pumped ashore for the Ipswich Chemical Molasses Company Ltd. Whilst discharging, the crew painted the rails and strake until at 10.30 p.m. they were ready to leave Ipswich for the passage down the coast for King's Lynn.

Photographed the day *Prowess* arrived at Ipswich, the *Archibald Russell*, her hull, scarred and rust pocked by nearly four months at sea, is almost completely repainted for her return voyage to the far side of the world.

Prowess was back alongside Gregory's Wharf, King's Lynn at 4.40 p.m. on Tuesday 23rd May to await the next morning's tide to warp the ship off to mooring buoys in the river, there to await the critical moment to get under way to go under the bridge to load molasses again, for Ipswich. A third freight was loaded on Monday 29th but when it was time came to get away the chief engineer reported trouble - a cracked cylinder head - so they warped down to Gregory's to order a spare part, which arrived next morning. The crew assisted in getting the engine part aboard and by 11.50 a.m. the *Prowess* was ready to proceed on passage for Ipswich, picking up he firm's sailing

Cromer lighthouse was first lit in 1680, the present light commissioned in 1830 as coastal erosion, still a problem today, dictated retreat from the cliff edge.

barge *Martha* in tow at 12.30. After passing Cromer Light the sailing barge broke adrift and was left to her own devices; *Prowess* carried on at full speed for Cliff Quay to discharge.

A fourth freight was loaded at the King's Lynn beet sugar refinery wharf after the two day Whitsun holiday, finishing midday on Wednesday 7th June when the ship was prepared for sea, with orders for Bergen op Zoom, Holland, instead of Ipswich. *Prowess* left Lynn in charge of a Pilot at 6 p.m. to pass the Blakeney Bell Buoy at midnight and set a course south-east by east. Thick fog set in and the ship slowed to pass a naval vessel testing her guns, firing at a floating target in tow. They resumed full speed when the fog cleared just before midday and at 7.50 p.m. passed into the Veerse Gat anchorage and let go 15 fathoms before arriving at their destination when the tide served. A further six similar passages, loaded on 7th, 13th and 29th June, 4th, 17th and 24th July, were completed when *Prowess* arrived at Bergen op Zoom on 27th to discharge and complete this series of trips from King's Lynn.

On 2nd August *Prowess* returned to Purfleet for bunkering and on 5th August had two lifeboats placed on board before leaving Greenhithe for Cantley where *Prowess* arrived on August Bank Holiday, Monday, 7th August, to load and leave bound for Bergen op Zoom again where, on arrival, she berthed alongside Spiritusfabriek wharf.

Prowess returned to Cantley to load on Monday 14th August to repeat the trip, but the following evening there was a short in the starboard electric light and shortly after passing the Middle Steen Bank light buoy the main engine stopped. The engineer reported that fuel had been 'watered' and they stopped for 35 minutes, before getting going again and arriving at Bergen op Zoom on a falling tide, where they grounded in the main channel at 1.30 p.m., refloating at

The underwater lines of *Prowess* were revealed after she ran aground whilst attempting to reach the Bergen op Zoom berth at Nedalco Spiritusfabriek.

11.20 p.m. that night and mooring alongside at midnight. *Prowess* discharged on Thursday 17th, returning to Cantley to load, again for Bergen on 23rd, where she was ordered to proceed to King's Lynn. This involved going through the unrigging procedure at Gregory's Wharf in order to get access to moor alongside the King's Lynn refinery jetty, where they were to spend four days cleaning the tanks one by one and loading molasses. *Prowess* left the berth, got clear of the bridges and departed at 4 p.m. on 1st September to discharge at Bergen op Zoom on the 4th, before returning to the firm's Greenhithe yard for repairs.

The crew were cleaning the tanks and 'keeping the time of the yard' from Tuesday 5th until Saturday, when the ship returned, having run trials all day. On Sunday 17th more engineers came aboard for more trials and the crew spent the rest of the day ostensibly washing, cleaning and drying the tanks, a turn of phrase perhaps sometimes used to cover idle periods for the crew.

On Monday 18th September the ship was sent to bunker at Purfleet, with *Co-operator* in tow, to lie alongside *Acclivity*. Next day *Prowess* proceeded at full speed to Holehaven where she came alongside a Russian tanker to load cotton oil and take two dumb barges alongside, presumably also loaded with oil, before returning to Greenhithe. *Prowess* was then ordered to Thames Haven with the two barges and then to undertake some 'river work', probably to prove her repairs satisfactory close to home, The crew scrubbed out the tanks ready for inspection in readiness for loading petroleum spirit.

Eventually the tank inspector turned up aboard. He must have been satisfied, for at 10.20 a.m. *Prowess* proceeded to Coryton Spirit Jetty to load. The petroleum spirit was finished loading at 2.20 p.m. and *Prowess* had orders for Exeter. By 10.30 p.m. they were abeam Dover Pier; 1.30 on Sunday morning 1st October found them off Dungeness; at 5.15 a.m. off Beachy Head; 2.55 p.m. at the Needles and 9.00 Portland Bill was to starboard, the wind north-easterly with moderate to poor visibility. At 2.45 a.m. on Monday morning *Prowess* brought up at anchor awaiting daylight in the River Exe estuary. A Pilot came aboard at 6.15 a.m. to guide the ship to Turf Lock where she arrived at 7.50 and cleared at 8.20 into the Exeter Ship Canal for the four mile journey to the Double Locks before going alongside the Trinidad Oil Jetty at 11.50 a.m. An hour later pipe lines were connected to discharge the cargo of spirit. Once emptied, the pipes were disconnected at 11 p.m.

Years later Capt. Charlie Fielder recalled 'I myself have done many petrol cargoes when in the *Prowess*. When in port you was not allowed to pump out after dark unless you were granted permission and that only to drain tanks to complete discharge. You had to have special hand lamps for this, encased in leather. I myself [was] caught by [an] inspector using an ordinary torch at Exeter. He was very severe with me, only I'd the proper torch close to me and explained the battery had suddenly given out and he let one go without a summons. Many skippers I know was very apprehensive about [petroleum] cargoes as especially when there was a heavy thunder and lightening storm but we just put the copper wire overboard from the mast head conductor.'

The passage to Northam, Southampton started with swinging the ship at 6.35 a.m. on Tuesday 3rd October to arrive at Turf Lock at 8.15 to pick up a Pilot, clear the lock at 8.40 to proceed for Exmouth, dropping the Pilot at Exmouth Pier. Then at around 10 a.m. the ship was ballasted down for the sea passage. Portland Bill was abeam at 4 p.m., and after passing the Needles at 8.15 p.m., the ballast water was discharged whilst underway. *Prowess* anchored off the River Hamble entrance in Southampton Water at 10.10 but was under way again at 6.50 a.m. to turn into the River Itchen and arrive off Anglo's wharf at Northam at 7.45 a.m. to start loading.

Paraffin oil, 60 cans of petrol and 90 crates of Essolube was loaded before *Prowess* left for Newport, Isle of Wight at 12.30 p.m. Arriving at 2.50 p.m., she was unable to berth on the ebb tide and ordered to await the next high water. On Thursday 5th October,

A view down river at Newport, Isle of Wight. The Anglo depot moved in the 1930s from the west quay (left) to Seaclose Quay (far right), where storage tanks away from the river were served by pipelines.

when the ship floated, she was moved and moored in the berth. Discharge was completed at 3 p.m. the same day.

Prowess dropped down off the berth, turned and proceeded down the River Medina, through Cowes, and full ahead for Coryton. The firm's sailing barge *Greenhithe* was taken in tow at 5.30; Beachy Head light passed that evening at 11.30 and the barge cast off half an hour after passing the Dungeness Light at 3.45 a.m. on Friday 6th October. *Prowess* berthed alongside at Coryton at 1.25 p.m., loaded

90 tons of spirit and 80 tons of 'special' spirit and was away on a return passage to Woolston, Southampton at 5 p.m. She moored alongside the Regent Wharf there 24 hours later and was ordered to discharge on Monday morning.

The return trip on 9th October was to be a passage to Cantley, for further work in the molasses trade. For the next three months or so *Prowess* and *Saunter* were to be engaged in lightering molasses from Cantley to the larger steamships of the fleet berthed below the bridge at Yarmouth. The two ships were also towing the Everard sailormen through the bridges. *Alf Everard* was ready one Thursday evening but *Prowess* was ordered to wait for *Fred Everard*. Owing to rain she was not loaded in time to make the daylight passage down river. *Greenhithe* and *Cambria* were also towed to Yarmouth North Quay. *Prowess* went back

Aboard Everard's *Greenhithe* under sail.

Cantley's tanks are prominent between factory and a considerable length of river frontage.

again to Cantley for further cargo for *Asperity* discharging into her at Gt. Yarmouth on 1st November.

Then, a perhaps welcome change, the crew set to cleaning out tanks ready for a peanut oil cargo from Selby. Weather conditions deteriorated overnight, calling for the ballasting of the ships tanks and the M.V. *Annuity* arrived to lie alongside. They remained

Saunter was a former Admiralty X lighter, converted to a motor tanker She is seen here at Bergen op Zoom, when owned by Everard.

weatherbound for two days with the crew taking the opportunity to rig a new derrick topping lift, taking down the 'union' screws on both port and starboard shrouds, greasing and covering the threads for weather protection. The gale abated to enable them to get under way at 9 a.m. on Saturday 4th November to anchor above Spurn light, inside the Humber, that evening. Under way at 4.10 a.m. a Hull Pilot was picked up for Goole where the Trent Pilot came aboard at 8.13 and they arrived at Selby, mooring alongside to clean the tanks and start loading at 11.30. The cargo, 220 tons of peanut oil for Jurgens Wharf, Purfleet, was discharged in four and a half hours on Wednesday 8th November. Fuel was bunkered at Anglo's Wharf and the ship returned to Greenhithe.

Sailing barges were often towed to speed their passage - here the *Lady Mary*, sails set on a windless day, is at anchor awaiting a 'pluck', a fair tide, or a bit of breeze.

While cleaning the tanks and moving alongside the barge roads the skipper was taken ill and ordered ashore. The work continued with assistance from the crew of *Agility* whose skipper took charge for the time being, but on Monday orders were received to leave with S.B. *Lady Mary* in tow for Cantley and Norwich with the skipper of the steamer *Tartary* taking charge.

He had an uneventful passage, loading on Wednesday and Thursday returning to Yarmouth on Friday 17th November to discharge into *Asperity* on Saturday and return with a further load on Tuesday. At 3.15 p.m. that day orders were received to proceed to sea to search for the sailing barge *Ethel Everard*, but it was not until 3.15 a.m. the next day that the cargo had been discharged at Yarmouth and *Prowess* was able to go looking for the barge, pumping water ballast aboard as she went. Abreast of Dunwich at 10.15 they received reports that the barge had arrived at Gt. Yarmouth and so they turned back. The ballast was discharged and at 1.40 p.m. they entered Yarmouth Piers and picked up *Ethel Everard* in tow for Cantley.

On Thursday 23rd November Charlie Fielder helped *Saunter* let go from the loading berth, and *Prowess* took her place to load. Finished at 7.25 the following morning, *Prowess* got under way for Yarmouth to moor alongside *Saunter* on Jewson's wharf to await the S.S. *Asperity*. She arrived at 5 p.m. to berth at South Quay and connect her steam pipes to start the transfer on Saturday. The transshipment of the next cargo to *Asperity* did not proceed without incident, first the shore pipe line burst within an hour of starting to load, then the return was delayed as the main engine gave trouble and this was followed by the ship grounding in Breydon Water at 2 p.m. The tide started to flood and half an hour later *Prowess* refloated and went through Yarmouth Bridge to moor alongside *Asperity* at 3.10 p.m. The discharge was completed at 5.30 next morning, Wednesday 5th December and, with the sailing barges *Martha*, *Hibernia* and *Will Everard* in tow, *Prowess* passed through Yarmouth Bridge only to receive orders

The *Ethel Everard* (left) with another barge alongside, leaves Gt. Yarmouth under tow of the tug *Tactful*.

to stop and await the *Fred Everard* next morning to join the tow. The sight of the tanker, just 20 feet longer than her four charges astern, must have been quite a spectacle.

Prowess continued the lightering between Cantley and Gt. Yarmouth to *Asperity* until the end of the year. On the way back to Cantley on 13th December they found that the firm's M.V. *Grit* had been blown ashore above Reedham village, but *Prowess* was unable to pull her off owing to high winds. Further cargoes were loaded on the 14th, 19th, 20th and 23rd and the sailing barges *Lady Mary*, *Alf Everard* and *Scot* were towed one way or the other until Christmas Eve, when *Prowess* returned to Cantley. She spent time alongside the jetty to wait until Wednesday 28th for a further load to *Asperity*, to discharge overnight, return, load again, discharge on 30th, and return to moor alongside Cantley loading jetty to await the New Year.

Whether or not the crew celebrated either Christmas or New Year aboard or at home is not recorded, but Monday 1st January 1934 saw *Prowess* loading more molasses at Cantley to discharge to *Asperity*. While proceeding down the lower reaches of the river with S.B. *Royalty* in tow *Prowess* collided with the M.V. *River Witham* of Hull, resulting in slight damage to the starboard bulwark. The tow was cast off after passing though Yarmouth Bridge and she moored outside *Saunter* at the South Quay to await the arrival of *Asperity* from Antwerp. That did not happen until Thursday 11th at 4.45 a.m. before *Prowess* dropped alongside. The steam pipe was connected, the cargo of molasses steamed and discharged, then the pump washed out, before the bridge was opened at 7.00 a.m. for *Prowess* to return to Cantley to reload. Two hours and ten minutes saw them back at the sugar factory where the pipes were fitted for loading and the crew found time to polish the brasswork in the wheelhouse. Loaded by 3.10 p.m., the ship was shifted to let *Saunter* onto the berth, before leaving for Gt. Yarmouth.

There was more of the same, back and forth to Cantley, load after load, with more towage thrown in for good measure. Having worked in the river for three months, the master received instructions on Saturday 20th January, 1934 to load and prepare for sea and make passage for Bergen op Zoom. On arrival, after clearing customs they moored alongside to discharge at 4.30 p.m. Saturday and on the Monday the log reads '11.15 a.m., full speed for Cantley, England'. Back at Gt. Yarmouth they cleared customs and received orders to tow *Lady Mary*, bound for Norwich. *Prowess* discharged her ballast water from tanks 4 then 3 as she passed through Reedham Bridge at 12.15.

Prowess occupies the alongside berth at Bergen op Zoom with *Tartary* outside her.

The tow was cast off for Colman's at Carrow Bridge where, at the top end of the river, the ship was turned with a slight mishap, breaking the 'union' screw[4] spindle on the foremast stay. *Prowess* moored alongside Boulton & Paul's, and next morning fitted a spare screw and cleaned the brasswork again while waiting for the sailorman to finish unloading.

They left with *Lady Mary* in tow at 9.15 a.m. through Thorpe Road Bridge at 4.30 p.m. to moor alongside until Thursday morning, stopped by darkness and thick fog. Back down at Cantley, they loaded molasses and received orders to tow *Lady Mary* to Gt. Yarmouth, where further orders instructed the tow to continue to Harwich. On Saturday morning they got under way at 6.15 a.m., passing Orfordness at 12.55 to cast off the tow at 3.30 p.m. and proceed on passage to Bergen op Zoom overnight. *Prowess* anchored in the entrance to Bergen op Zoom Creek to await the morning flood on Sunday 28th January.

Bergen op Zoom and the works of the Zuid-Nederlandsche Melasse-Spritusfabriek, or Z.N.M.S for short, where *Prowess* and other Everard tankers delivered their cargoes.

[4.] 'Union' screw; another name for bottlescrew or turnbuckle.

Prowess moored alongside *Acclivity* at 1.35 p.m. to await her turn to discharge, which came on Wednesday, using the onshore steam injectors and pumps. The discharge started in the early hours and was completed at 11.00, the shore men then able to wash out the tanks. The crew fitted the ballast water pump and they were under way at 4 p.m. for Zierikzee Pier for customs clearance. They did not get far, anchoring half-a-mile off with the wind increasing.

The anchor dragged overnight on so they had to get under way to let go the port anchor out with thirty fathoms of chain, the crew clearing the starboard anchor cable of turns, then cleaning out the chain locker and restowing the chain. *Prowess* remained windbound until at 1.20 p.m. the weather had improved sufficiently to proceed to sea on passage for Cantley. At Gt. Yarmouth Bridge she joined *Assiduity* and took aboard some 500 gallons of fuel oil before getting under way for the Cantley loading jetty, where she arrived on Saturday. Sunday was a day of rest, loading being planned for Monday.

Prowess alongside at Bergen op Zoom. February 1934 was *Prowess* and Charlie's last visit there, other Dutch destinations to the fore in the years to come.

Tuesday 6th February saw *Prowess* moor alongside The London & Rochester Trading Company's sailing barge *Pudge* at Wenn's Wharf, Gt. Yarmouth, before leaving for an overnight passage to Bergen op Zoom to discharge and get beneaped! Needless to say the log records the ongoing hard work of the crew, scrubbing below the waterline during the enforced stay. Afloat again, it was to Coryton she sailed to load gas oil for Weymouth, arriving there

on the 12th. Passing though Weymouth Bridge, it was clear that there was insufficient water for the berth.

They were unable to get alongside until 14th February to discharge for the gas works. That same evening they disconnected, got the gangway aboard, warped her head round across to the western quay to pass back through the bridge. Off the Needles Light at 12.25, they looked in the Solent for the *Royalty* to take her in tow, but she was not seen. Dense fog made them anchor in West Bay, Dungeness, but they were under way again at 10 a.m. to round the Foreland to anchor below the Mid Blyth buoy in yet more dense fog. The water ballast was discharged and *Prowess*, in much better visibility, arrived at Greenhithe on Saturday morning.

On Monday 19th orders were received for Erith Oil Works to pick up 20 empty barrels for the S.S. *Glenogle*. She entered the Royal Albert Dock with two tank barges in tow to load soya bean oil but had to shift to a lay-by berth because of the non-arrival of the correct paperwork, which was not forthcoming until Wednesday morning. Taking more empty barrels and 4 full casks of soya bean oil and towing three tank barges, *Prowess* was under way from the dock locks by 2 p.m. down river to Erith Oil Works. Two of the tank barges were handed over to the firm's tug *Faverolle* and on Thursday morning pipelines were connected from ship to shore to discharge the bean oil. By 1 p.m. both *Prowess* and the tank barge *Southward* were ready to leave Erith for Greenhithe where the ship received orders to leave for Coryton at 6 a.m. next day.

On Friday 23rd February *Prowess* first tied alongside *Capable* to off-load the empty barrels to the former auxiliary schooner which the firm were soon to sell. It was not until 10 a.m. that the ship was able to leave Coryton Jetty to load 150 tons of gas oil for the Channel Islands. She was ready to depart at 6.25 p.m. but off the East Blyth buoy they ran into dense fog and anchored. The fog did not lift until 2 p.m. on Saturday when they got under way.

There was engine trouble at 10 a.m. which forced *Prowess* to stop while it was sorted out. After half-an-hour the engine was restarted for just ten minutes, before it was stopped again. The engine restarted at 11.15 p.m., the passage continuing until 3.40 a.m. on Monday 26th, when they picked up a Pilot outside the entrance to St. Helier Harbour who took them alongside the quay near the electric light works to prepare to discharge their gas oil. The crew made bass rope fenders which were needed, as were the bass rope springs which were put out to cope with the Channel Islands 40 feet plus tidal range, one of the world's biggest.

Before setting off, ballast water was pumped into the tanks but strong winds and heavy seas outside the harbour prevented sailing on Tuesday and Wednesday, while the crew occupied their time cleaning the brasswork, portholes etc. They were able to leave St. Helier Harbour at 4.15 p.m. on Thursday 1st March 1934 to drop the Pilot and proceed full speed for Greenhithe.

The engine was stopped for forty minutes owing to water contamination in the main fuel tank, but by 1.24 a.m. on Friday Beachy Head was abeam and at 5.50 *Prowess* was at anchor in West Bay, Dungeness, in dense fog. This cleared somewhat by 8 that morning to allow them to get under way again and by 4.30 p.m. they were pumping out the ballast water off Grain Spit and washing out the tanks. *Prowess* moored on a ship buoy at Greenhithe at 8.10 p.m. on Friday 2nd March and pumped out her main fuel tank into the *Co-operator* to locate the leak.

The crew took the opportunity to wipe out the main cargo tanks before *Prowess* moved to moor 3rd bottom off the shipyard. Riveters were at work in the bottom of the tank which, repairs completed, passed inspection on Tuesday morning. They took on fuel, water and lubricating oil from the *Co-operator* so that the ship was ready at 5 p.m. to leave Greenhithe for her next cargo.

One of the big mooring buoys off the Everard yard. Nearest the shore is a tank barge, outside her the barge *Capstan*, then the *Co-operator* with the sailing barge *Nellie Mary*. At the river end is the *Stonebow* with the tug *F.T. Everard*, second of that name, approaching the trot.

Her destination Zaandam, Holland, *Prowess* left at 5.00 p.m. on Tuesday 6th March, taking on ballast water on the way, passing the Nore at 7.35, the Girdler at 8.45 and the Tongue at 9.53. The ship crossed into Dutch waters, recording the North Hinder Light at 3.05 a.m. and five minutes later they picked up the Dutch Pilot for Ijmuiden Lock, at the entrance to the North Sea Canal. The water ballast was discharged on their way to Zaandam lock with a canal Pilot for the Hague Oil Mills. There *Prowess* loaded linseed oil, then returned to the Thames and delivered their cargo on Saturday 10th to Mellish's Wharf, Millwall.

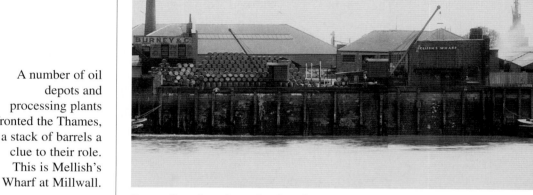

A number of oil depots and processing plants fronted the Thames, a stack of barrels a clue to their role. This is Mellish's Wharf at Millwall.

Just after leaving the berth *Prowess* suffered a slight impact with the dumb barge *Bessie* in tow of the steam tug *Sandwich* owned by Jacobs Lighterage of Deptford, but no damage was reported. She was then under way back across the North Sea, this time to Druyps Mills, Zaandam, reached on 13th March where she loaded more linseed oil, including 55 tons from two small barges, but strong winds left her windbound from Thursday until Sunday 18th March.

The Master decided to put back to Ijmuiden Harbour where they remained awaiting a break in the weather, which came on Tuesday 20th. They left the sea locks for London with the wind fining away and rain showers all day. *Prowess* berthed at Rotherhithe, discharged, cleaned tanks and returned to Greenhithe where orders were received to proceed to the Anglo American Jetty at Purfleet to load 200 tons of 'patching oil' for Dundee.

She sailed at 1.25 p.m. on Saturday 24th March to pick up the Tay Pilot at 8.45 p.m. on Monday at the Tay Bar Buoy where they had minor mechanical trouble, stopping the engine. At 9.40 p.m. they arrived to await in a cutting for level water at Dundee Docks. Next day the tanks were discharged, wiped clean, the ship ballasted and ordered to Hull Docks on the midday tide on Wednesday. They anchored half a mile above the Middle light buoy, the ballast was discharged and at 3.15 p.m. *Prowess* arrived at British Extract Mills to await a berth there, after some barges had left on the tide.

Good Friday was taken as a holiday but next day the shore men connected pipelines to load 200 tons of soya bean oil for London. The ship was under way at 6.10 p.m. down the River Hull under pilotage before running at full speed overnight to arrive off Erith Oil Works at midnight on Easter Sunday, 1st April. At 12.35 she moored on the inside of the jetty there, alongside a dumb barge, to await orders. The log reads 'This day being a National Bank Holiday no other work being done'. However, for at least one member of the crew there was some urgency to return home.

On Bank Holiday Monday, 2nd April 1934, Charles Henry Fielder, bachelor, aged 30 years, a seaman in the mercantile marine, of 110 Riverside Gardens, Hammersmith, married 28 year old Ada Edith Owen who, with two young children, was two years the widow of Thomas Frederick Owen, of 73 Riverside Gardens. Ada's father Joseph Pruden, a contractor's carman, had died but another Pruden was one of the witnesses to the ceremony before an assistant registrar in Hammersmith Registry Office. Charles took up residence at Flat 73, but Charlie Fielder was only too soon to be back on board *Prowess*.

The Marriage Certificate for Charlie and Ada Fielder.

No.	When Married	Name and Surname	Age	Condition	Rank or Profession	Residence at the time of Marriage	Father's Name and Surname	Rank or Profession of Father
94	Second April 1934	Charles Henry Fielder	30 years	Bachelor	Seaman Mercantile Marine	110 Riverside Gardens Hammersmith	Charles Fielder	Bargeman
		Ada Edith Owen	28 years	Widow	-	73 Riverside Gardens Hammersmith	Joseph John Pruden (deceased)	Contractors Carman

1934. Marriage solemnized at The Register Office in the District of Hammersmith in the County of Metropolitan Borough of Hammersmith

Married in the Register Office according to the Rites and Ceremonies of the _____ by Licence before _____ by mo, N. Nicholls Registrar

This Marriage was solemnized between us, C. H. Fielder / A. E. Owen — In the Presence of us, E. C. Pruden / E. M. Howard — N M Thompson Superintendent Registrar

After the 1934 Easter Bank Holiday and his marriage, Charlie Fielder immediately returned to *Prowess*, still at Erith Oil Works jetty. There was no mention of that fact, or of his absence, noted in the working log. What was of concern to those on board on Tuesday 3rd April was the lack of available tank space at the jetty. The crew spent the next few days chipping and painting but eventually at 8.35 on Thursday morning capacity became available and they were able to commence discharge of the soya bean oil.

Suddenly, at 12.30 p.m., orders were received to stop unloading, with instructions to re-load the 30 tons already discharged and proceed to Jurgens Jetty, Purfleet, to discharge the cargo into tanks there [probably because the oil was contaminated with water]. This was completed on Friday, when they returned to moor alongside the steaming barge off Greenhithe to wash out the tanks and get aboard a new steam coil to replace that in the No. 2 tank.

The ship remained alongside until Monday, when she moved to the Anglo-American Jetty at Purfleet to load lubricating oils for Hull. *Prowess* left at 11.45 a.m. to anchor in White Booth Roads in the River Humber at 7.30 next day, before moving to Seatons' Wharf to discharge on Thursday morning. Fifty tons of Bassa oil[1] had been discharged by 4.20 p.m.. so the 150 tons of red oil in tanks 3 and 4 had to be levelled to keep the ship on an even keel overnight. The red oil was discharged the following morning and the ship moved out of the Old Harbour to anchor in White Booth Roads in increasing winds. Water ballast was taken on but the ship remained weatherbound until Saturday, when they received orders to proceed to Zaandam to load linseed oil again.

Linseed oil is a golden-yellow edible oil obtained from crushed flax seeds. Its good drying properties made it suitable for use as a basic raw material in varnish, oil paint, coatings and linoleum production. It was also used by Lever Brothers for margarine production during W.W.I. Dutch companies Jurgens and Van den Bergh merged in 1927 to form the Margarine Union which, on 2nd September 1929 merged with Lever Brothers to create Unilever, to develop and market both margarine and soaps. Their wharves at

[1] Bassa Oil Ltd is a Cameroon based edible oil manufacturer.

Purfleet were almost opposite the Everard yard at Greenhithe and it was only to be expected that the barge-owners should develop craft to transport the oil used in Unilever products in bulk. The tanks had to be scrupulously clean as the oil could not be contaminated by rust particles or by seawater, otherwise it would be rejected, compensation sought and disposal of the contaminated cargo would become a costly problem for the ship-owner. The tanks also had to be filled as full as possible, taking into account expansion, so that as little space as possible is left above the cargo. Any change in its consistency during transportation could be irreversible, so the oil had to be kept liquid. During the voyage and whilst loading, travelling and pumping the temperature of the oil had to be precisely controlled. Pumping could be difficult in cold weather, hence the need to heat the cargo and the development of specialist craft, such as *Prowess*.

Jacob Vis pioneered the Zaan oil industry, his premises in 1900, above, were wind powered, and below seen in *Prowess's* day.

Everard tankers regularly crossed the north sea to wharves in Holland to load linseed oil from the Dutch associates of Unilever for delivery to plants in the U.K. Many of the factories processing the oil were on the River Zaan which ran 10 kilometres through the municipality of Zaanstad (Zaan City) north of Amsterdam from West-Knollendam in the north, past Koog aan de Zaan to Zaandam in the south, an area believed to be the world's first industrial region. The river became an arm of the Noordseekanaal, the ship canal which had been cut by an English contractor between 1865 and November 1876 from Ijmuiden to Amsterdam.

The river had been open to the Zuiderzee until 1872 when the Orange Locks were built. With the completion of these locks the North Sea Canal was no longer tidal and a consistent water level could be maintained. At the western end, the canal drained into the North Sea through the Spui Locks at Ijmuiden which were augmented by the largest pumping station in Europe, vital to the groundwater management of the western Netherlands. The small set of locks 'Zuidersluis' 110m long by 11m wide and 3.5m deep and the 'South Locks' 110m x 20m x 8m were built at the mouth in 1876 where the new town of Ijmuiden developed as a major port. In 1896 the Middensluis (Middle Locks) were built 225m x 25m x 10m followed in 1929 by the Noordersluis (North Locks) which at 400m x 50m x 15m were Europe's largest locks at that time.

The Younghusband, Barnes & Co. Ltd. Thames-side wharf with the tell-tale pile of barrels and, centre of picture, two vertical oil storage tanks.

The cargo which *Prowess* loaded at Zaandam on 16th April was for Younghusband, Barnes & Co.Ltd of Lower King and Queen Wharf in Rotherhithe Street. The firm refined vegetable oils for use in paints and occupied a somewhat ramshackle wharf just downstream of the extensive wharves of Bellamy's Wharf & Dock Co. Ltd. whose 350 foot long jetty allowed ships of up to 13,000 tons to discharge at all states of the tide while coasters, barges and lighters could take the ground alongside the river frontage wharves. During the discharge on 18th April, the engineer discovered that coupling bolts on the pump gearbox were in danger of breaking, so pumping was stopped while temporary repairs were made and the unloading could completed next day.

The ship returned to Greenhithe for spares and victualling, leaving for Zaandam at 7.50 p.m., to anchor for the night off Yantlet Creek, reaching her destination on Sunday 22nd April. She had loaded and cleared the sea lock for London on Monday but, at 4.40 a.m. on Tuesday, after having passed the Maas Lightvessel, the skipper decided to turn back as the ship was making little headway in heavy weather. She went back through the ship lock to moor alongside the canal bank at Ijmuiden where she remained until Saturday 28th. Underway again at 5.16 a.m., there was slight engine trouble at 9.35 a.m. with the bilge pump letting water into the bilges. The valves were choked, and to clear them the engine had to be stopped until the problem was solved. They resumed full speed for London at 10.15 a.m. and at 4.20 a.m. on Sunday morning *Prowess* had anchored above the Jenkin Buoy in Sea Reach before proceeding to Rotherhithe to discharge the linseed oil.

There was insufficient tank capacity ashore so pumping had to stop for the day. They started again on 1st May, when the screw bolts on the pump gearbox finally broke, so a shore pump was pressed into service and work was resumed to finish at 5.35 p.m. The ship then returned to Greenhithe to spend the next day cleaning her tanks for the next cargo, and to take on more stores.

Four grades of lubricating oil from Purfleet to Hull was next, which was pumped ashore on Tuesday 8th May. *Prowess* was then ordered to Knollendam where, it being Ascension Day and a public holiday in Holland, loading a cargo of linseed oil was deferred until Friday. They were still able to clear the Ijmuiden Locks at 7.05 p.m. the same day with orders for Greenhithe, to discharge overside into the barge *Outward*, on Monday 14th May. With more linseed oil to load at Knollendam, they were under way at 4.30 p.m. to anchor off Broadstairs because of the increasing north-westerly wind. Nevertheless they arrived there on Wednesday and sailed laden for Rotherhithe late on Friday to discharge after the Whit-Monday holiday.

Linseed oil had largely replaced the regular carriage of molasses. *Prowess* was ordered to Mason's Oil Wharf, Ipswich, anchoring below Pin Mill on Wednesday evening. Loading took all day Thursday. Next day the ship moved to Cliff Quay for fresh water before sailing for Rotherhithe, but it was not until Monday 28th May that the cargo was discharged after which the ship moved to Greenhithe for 'engine works' and the fitting of a new windlass gypsy. At tide time on Wednesday S.S. *Asperity* arrived and orders to sail for Zaandam were received. *Prowess* picked up S.B. *Scot* in tow at 3.50 a.m. on Thursday morning for three hours until, off Shoeburyness she was cast off. They arrived at 9.30 a.m. next morning, loaded and passed out of the Ijmuiden Locks to temporarily moor alongside one of the firm's ships when they got back to Greenhithe on Saturday 2nd June.

Then followed another cargo of linseed oil to Rotherhithe, followed on 8th June by a delivery of linseed oil to the Greenwich Inlaid Linoleum Works at Tunnel Road on the Greenwich peninsular. Linoleum was the brainchild of Frederick Walton from Manchester who was probably one of the most prolific and influential inventors and industrialists of the late Victorian era. Walton himself coined the word 'linoleum' from the Latin 'linus' (flax) and 'oleum' (oil). He found that his new material, using finely ground cork waste, resins and gums, oxidised linseed oil, plus colouring matter, could be rolled out onto a base of woven jute. He took out a lease on what became Victoria Wharf, to house a machine that he had designed to make inlaid, or mosaic linoleum.

Its practicalities were soon appreciated; it was durable, sturdy and clean and could be produced in all sorts of designs. The company was taken over by Michael Nairn of Kirkcaldy in 1922 and the Greenwich factory became very prosperous. Greenwich Inlaid Linoleum was the standard geometrical pattern fashionable at the time and some specialist lino was made, including a design for Lyons teashops with their logotype in it.

Charlie Fielder and *Prowess* were back alongside the Knollendam factory on Thursday 14th June loading another 200 tons of linseed oil for the Linoleum Works. Pumping commenced at 6.30 a.m. and loading finished at 11.40 a.m. They waited for the canal Pilot to sail to Zaandam for Ijmuiden where the ship locked out at 5.40 p.m. A normal working day for the crew, but at 73 Riverside Gardens, Hammersmith, Ada Edith Fielder had given birth to June Doreen Fielder. It was not until Friday 6th July that Ada was able to register the birth, giving as the father's occupation, 'Able Seaman Mercantile Marine'.

The cargo from Knollendam was discharged at the Mellish's Sufferance Wharf, Millwall, after which the ship went to

Greenhithe for repairs on Monday 18th June. While there, on Wednesday 20th, the log reports 'crew unbending small sail from mast and unshipping sheathes[sic][2] from blocks and cleaning and getting in stores'. This is the only reference in the log of the ship carrying sail, although Ken Garrett recalls that when *Prowess* was used as a 'school ship' for newly promoted officers towards the end of her career, Capt. Harold Woods, a former deep-sea officer, was amazed when the crew set a rather tatty mainsail on the mast. However, on Thursday the tanks were recalibrated and in the evening they were underway to the Anglo American Jetty at Purfleet to bunker fuel oil, before sailing for Zaandam and a further cargo of linseed oil for Rotherhithe.

The Bull Fort, the larger of two defensive towers in the River Humber was built in W.W.I. but not finished before the war ended. It remains a conspicuous seamark near the White Booth Roads.

Orders for Cleveland Mill, Hull, to load two lots of 80 and 100 tons of cotton seed oil, were received on Friday 29th June. The ship was underway at 1 p.m. to anchor off the Bull Lightvessel in the Humber at 1.45 a.m. on Sunday morning, 1st July. After loading and clearing the old harbour entrance they anchored just after midnight at the White Booth Roads. When they came to restart the engine, the Engineer reported the main engine pump valves needed attention. At 4.30 a.m. on 3rd July *Prowess* got under way for London at reduced speed. She arrived off the Greenhithe barge roads at 10.30 a.m. next morning to discharge part of the cargo into the barges *Lea* and *Diamond*. At 4.30 p.m. the ship went to bunker at the Anglo American Oil Wharf at Purfleet and leave for John Knight's Wharf at Silvertown where they berthed at 7 p.m. It was noted that the weather was 'rather warm'. Next morning they started to discharge the remaining 100 ton of cotton oil to the shore and then returned to Greenhithe, where *Prowess* moored alongside S.S. *Asperity* at 7.20 p.m. The crew set to washing out the tanks and three hours later the ship was on its way to Zaandam.

Prowess arrived at 1.30 a.m. on Saturday 7th July where she moored to a dolphin, waiting eight hours for Customs clearance for Knollendam. Two hours later they were alongside the factory but were not to be loaded until Monday, so the crew put

[2.] Mispelt 'sheaves', the pully wheels within a block.

the two lifeboats overboard. It was still rather warm and Sunday was a holiday with no work being done, but the log makes no mention of the activities of the crew or where the boats were taken, or whether the opportunity was taken just to keep them watertight in the summer heat. The boats were brought back on board on Monday while they were taking on 220 tons of linseed oil to give the ship a draught of 7'8" at the bow and 8'3" aft. They were underway at 1.15 p.m. and alongside Everard's *Aridity* on Greenwich Buoys at 7.15 p.m. next day.

The *Ramble* seen passing through Reedham swing bridge, the vessel ahead clearing a way through the frozen river. Note the foresail and gaff mainsail to give an extra knot when the wind served.

Prowess was ordered to Rotherhithe to discharge and returned to Greenhithe to lay for the evening alongside the former Admiralty X lighter motor tanker *Ramble*, one of six Pollock designed 'Beetles' built for the Dardanelles campaign, that the company had acquired. Next morning, Saturday 14th July at 4.30 a.m. they proceeded to Zaandam to load a further 203 tons for Rotherhithe which was discharged on Thursday, after which the ship returned to Greenhithe for repairs. Further work on *Prowess* was deemed necessary, so on Monday she was put ashore alongside the M.V. *Heather Pet*[3] on the ship repair yard.

[3] *Heather Pet* was a wooden motor coaster built in 1921 by Wills & Packham, known for their sailing barges. When in Everard ownership she was initially renamed *Assurity*.

Repairs continued and the decision was made to pay off the crew on Saturday 28th July. Charlie Fielder left for a short stay in the M.V. *Actuosity*, leaving her on Monday 13th August. This turned out to be a good move as in the following November her main engine crankshaft seized off Illfracombe.

Most of her crew had served in sailing ships and were able to jury rig some sails using the hatch tarpaulins, but she was nevertheless driven ashore.

Charlie's diary only has the word '*Actuosity*' for the first part of August, but he also included some informative press cuttings. 'British Tanker in Collision' is the heading for a two inch long cutting from an unidentified newspaper reporting that during the night *Prowess* was involved in a collision

Actuosity, like the earlier *Prowess*, was built for Everard by George Brown at Greenock in 1933. She survived the Ilfracombe stranding, but sank on 3rd October 1940 off Cromer, after striking a submerged object when bound from Newcastle to London with wheat.

outside Flushing harbour with the German steamer *Umeälv*, 1,293 tons, which had subsequently put into Dover for repairs. The *Prowess's* master, Capt. A. Seaman, was slightly hurt and a sailor, P. Atkinson, 'seriously injured' and taken to hospital. The ship succeeded in entering port, reported Reuters. Elsewhere the Dutch newspaper Algemeen Handelsblad of 7th December 1938 reported that the collision was in the dark at around 7.00 o'clock the previous evening, about twelve miles from the Noordhinder Lightvessel and that the worst injured had several broken ribs and was taken to Bethesda hospital, the *Prowess* having made it to Vlissingen under her own power. It is interesting to note that this collision took place after Charlie had left the *Prowess*, but its inclusion in his notebook would suggest he did not loose interest in the ship.

A much earlier collision, before Charlie shipped aboard, was thought to have taken place in 1931 when the *Prowess* was at anchor off Dungeness and she was hit by the Italian steamer *Capacitas* which was coming to anchor there. There turned out to be some doubt when the lawyers got involved as to whether the collision, or at least the claimed damage, had taken place there, for evidence was submitted that *Prowess* had subsequently collided with the Sandwich tollbridge and had sustained damage prior to the survey report was undertaken in respect of the first incident, making it impossible to apportion any claim.

Another lengthy press cutting in the Fielder diary at this point is part of a law report of an action concerning a collision between the *Chessington* and *Sedulity* which was at anchor,

although sheering about. The Everard ship was not built by George Brown in Greenock until 1936, so this cutting was not contemporaneous with Charlie Fielder's time in the *Prowess*.

Charlie returned to M.V. *Prowess*, lying off the firm's Greenhithe repair yard, on Monday 20th August 1934, when he was set to chipping and painting the overside hull. She was ready for engine trials on

Everard's *Sedulity*, photographed passing Rowhedge, on the River Colne, was engaged for many years delivering coal from the Humber to the Colchester Gas Works at Hythe Quay.

Tuesday and moved to a buoy off the yard. Next day the crew took in stores and left on passage for Zaandam, to arrive in the evening of Thursday 23rd. She was to load linseed oil again, indeed, apart from one cargo of gas oil from Purfleet to the British Gas Light Co. in Hull, this was to be the only kind of cargo for the rest of the year and beyond, until the October molasses 'season' of 1935.

The summer weather was variable with some thunderstorms, warm periods and usually light airs, although gale force winds in early October caused the ship to be windbound at Ijmuiden for some days. Passages to Rotherhithe, Millwall and Hull were interspersed with a couple of voyages to Dieppe on 11th October and 13th November, loading from railway tank wagons. On one voyage to Hull poor tides left *Prowess* stranded about ten foot off Seatons Wharf and she could only move a couple of feet nearer on the next tide. By this time the weather had deteriorated with storm force winds and the not uncommon dense fog, typical of the Humber.

On Wednesday 5th December *Prowess* left Greenhithe for the Anglo Jetty at Purfleet to load 200 tons of gas oil for Lowestoft. She anchored at 6.55 p.m. in the Yantlet in heavy rain squalls and a strong south-westerly wind but was under way at 1.40 a.m. to moor off the Anglo depot on Oulton Broad. The cargo was discharged at 9.15 p.m. and the ship took on ballast to depart for Greenhithe where she arrived at 9.55 p.m. on Friday. The ship went on the repair yard while the crew were steaming then drying the tanks and getting in stores on Saturday. Next day *Prowess* was ordered to Zaandam but turned back to Ramsgate Roads owing to bad weather. She remained at anchor until Monday evening when the ship proceeded slowly in dense fog, with lead soundings being taken, to arrive at Wormerveer on Tuesday morning to load more linseed oil.

She returned to Rotherhithe on Thursday 13th December to discharge part of the cargo to the barge *Victoria* as tank space ashore was not available until Saturday. The crew then set to clean the tanks while they lay on Charlton Buoys prior to loading the next cargo. This was to be gas oil from the S.S. *Olnal*, but she was delayed due to more dense fog in the river. *Prowess* was alongside her at 2.15 p.m. to load 200 tons for Hull. She arrived in the River Humber on Wednesday morning 19th December, to berth at the British Gas Light Co. wharf where the cargo was dipped and samples taken for checking, discharge commencing on Thursday morning. They were underway at 5.25 p.m. for Gt. Yarmouth to arrive alongside Palgrave Brown's quay on Friday 21st December at 10.30 that night. It is not clear if all the crew remained onboard over the Christmas holiday but the log mentions persistent thick fog during the period.

On Boxing Day the ship was ordered to get underway for Zaandam, at 6.40 p.m. passing down Yarmouth Haven, past Gorleston Piers at 7.00 and the Corton Light forty minutes later. She was across at Ijmuiden and alongside Koog aan Zaan quay to load on the evening of Thursday 27th. Loaded by Friday morning, *Prowess* departed at 2.20 p.m. to make the

Koog aan de Zaan, on the outskirts of Zaandam, is situated by a broad stretch of the River Zaan, industry lining the banks of this waterway which joins the North Sea Canal.

crossing in strong south-west winds, with the ship making heavy-weather of it and labouring. She went direct to Younghusband's Wharf, Rotherhithe, on Sunday to wait to discharge through her own pumps on Monday 31st December, 1934.

The Crew List for 1935 held in the National Maritime Museum was prepared by the master, T.C. Coker. aged 34, of Hamworthy, Dorset. C.H. Fielder is listed as mate while the deck crew were able seaman H.T.A. Pasley, aged 22, from Gt. Yarmouth and H.H. Morris, also 22, from nearby Somerton, as ordinary seaman and cook. The chief engineer was E.W. Cooper, 34, of Whitstable and his second engineer C. Reader from Norwich, aged 49. The list states that all the crew had served together the previous year on *Audacity*. Capt. Coker was about to be promoted and was succeeded on 18th January by Capt. George Douglas, aged 40, from Faversham. The Crew List also gives details of the weekly pay of each member of the Crew. The master received £6.0s.0d.; the mate £3.15s.0d. with the A.B. £2.15s.0d. and the O.S. £2.0s.0d. In the engine room the chief was paid £5.0s.0d. and his second £3.0s.0d. All the crew were responsible for their own food and as many voyages were only a day or so this might not seem unreasonable.

In the Memoranda page of the 1935 Boots Scribbling Diary are the compass courses seen from the Haisboro' Light to the Maplin Spit Buoy. Also given are the actual draught of water when light, fore 2'6", aft 7'6" and when fully loaded, fore 8'0" and aft 8'6" with the freeboard amidships, port and starboard when light 4'2" and fully loaded just eleven inches! The record for 1st January 1935 shows that *Prowess* resumed discharging cargo to the shore tanks at Greenhithe with several stoppages, later pumping the remainder aboard the barge *Upward*.

The first passage of the year was from Greenhithe to Wormerveer Fabriek, Holland, where Prowess loaded linseed oil for Hull. Capt. Coker anchored a quarter mile south of the Elbow Buoy, Scroby Sands, in a strong northerly wind with thirty fathoms of chain out and an anchor watch being kept. It was not until 9.30 p.m. on Wednesday 9th that, with a tug in attendance, she was alongside Seatons Wharf, discharging the 225 tons next day. They were underway down river at 10.45 p.m. on passage for Zaandam and another cargo for Rotherhithe. Fifty tons were discharged into the barge *Cowl* but then dense fog descended and the ship had to anchor on the north shore opposite Greenhithe for the night. The following day, Thursday 17th January, they were able to moor alongside Younghusband's Wharf to discharge 164 tons, leaving the rest to be pumped into the barge *Northward* a day later, when the new master, Capt. George Douglas took command.

The Everard premises in Greenhithe, a decade after the period of the narrative, are little changed, the shore tanks clear in the bottom right, one of their tank barges close by. They were known as the 'treacle tanks' to the yard men and Greenhithe villagers.

After taking on fuel at Purfleet, Capt Douglas stopped on the Greenhithe buoys for orders to proceed to Dieppe for linseed oil for Hull, returning light to Coryton to load 95 tons of gas oil for Weymouth. The log records the draught for this cargo at 5'6" fore, 6'3" aft. On reaching Dungeness East Bay the ship anchored in gale force winds, which prevailed all day on Friday 25th January, only getting under way next morning to report the starboard anchor chain had broken and its anchor lost. They continued on, recording the Horse Sands abeam at 10.15 a.m. and entering

Weymouth at 6.30 a.m. on Sunday. It seems the Gas Company could not provide a motor tanker lorry so they had to wait all Monday for the arrival of a one from London. As usual the crew were engaged in work about deck and painting overside the ship's hull, black. The lorry did not arrive until 4 p.m. on Tuesday, when they were able to start discharging into it, to shuttle the oil to the Gas Works, using the ship's pump. At 4.30 p.m. the lorry finished work and did not return until nine on Wednesday morning to take a further seven loads before finishing at 6.00 that evening. The ship left Portland Harbour at 6.45 p.m. to moor alongside the hulk of the *Asian* to clean the tanks. *Prowess* then left for Zaandam, Holland, to load linseed oil for Rotherhithe and, once delivered went to Greenhithe to pick up new chain and an anchor. One is left wondering if the freight really paid its way.

Prowess left at 10.45 p.m. on Thursday 7th February for Zaandam, loading linseed oil again on the 11th, this time for Millwall, then again on 16th, following which she was weatherbound until Sunday 24th when she sailed for Seatons Wharf in Hull. In the 'Memoranda' section at the end of the diary there is a note 'Wednesday 27th Feb. 1935, while proceeding down River Hull had minor collision with keel *Thorne* of Hull, owners White of Hull, carrying a forward stanchion away off rails, slight damage to [keel's] timber heads caused by anchor flukes overhanging'

The next cargo loaded in Zaandam on 1st March was for Hull, returning light to Thameshaven on 7th to load Gas Oil for St. Helier, Jersey. The ship encountered snow squalls and heavy seas on passage, mooring alongside on Saturday 9th to discharge through a shore line. Steam to clean the tanks was supplied while they were weatherbound for another day.

In cold wintry weather the *Prowess* left the Channel Isles making slow progress in rough seas to Zaandam to load more linseed oil. The crew then had to work clearing debris to get at a sea water leak in the fo'c'stle of the ship. The oil loaded was for Younghusband's, Rotherhithe, which was discharged before the ship returned to Greenhithe at 1.34 a.m. on 20th March. Able Seaman Pasley and Ordinary Seaman Morris were discharged to be replaced by R.S. Walker and J.E. Jarvis, both from Gravesend,

Walker, aged 24, having served on *Alchymist* and Jarvis, aged 18, on the sailing barge *Hibernia*. Jarvis did not last long, being discharged at his own request in Hull on 8th April. With these alterations in her crew *Prowess* left at 1.20 p.m. for Zaandam on 20th March for more linseed oil destined for the Waterloo Mills in Hull. Returning to Holland she was weatherbound at Ijmuiden for the first week in April before making one further delivery.

On 12th April the logbook records 'ship unable to proceed on passage owing to main engine defects, ship's engineers trying to locate trouble; crew working about the ship painting fore-holds, sides and top.' The trouble was fixed by Monday 15th when the ship returned to Rotherhithe to discharge the linseed oil cargo and go to Greenhithe. She went alongside the tug/tender *Co-operator* to go on the ways for a survey after the Easter holiday weekend. Her lifeboats were taken ashore and one of her bottom plates was taken out, inspected and replaced. Charlie was able to return home to his wife and daughter.

After Easter, while the Company's directors considered the survey report, Charlie Fielder was employed on the steam tug *Faverolle* and as a lighterman on the dumb barge *Velocity* in Tilbury Dock

alongside the S.S. *Clan Monroe*. On Thursday 25th April the decision was taken to move *Prowess* to the slipways in Rochester. While the *Prowess* remained at Greenhithe the crew were sent to work chipping the tanks on the firm's S.S. *Tartary*. There was much concern when a large

Clan Line's *Clan Monroe* was built in 1918 and mined off Harwich in 1940 with the loss of 13 lives.

ship created an excessive wash whilst passing the berth and broke the mooring chains. Next day *Prowess* was floated off and remained alongside the wharf at Greenhithe until 30th April when she left, being towed by *Faverolle*, with the lighter *Revenge* alongside. She was placed on the slip at Doust & Co.'s Shipyard, Chatham, on 1st May, and hove up to the top of the slipway. Next day plates were cut out of her bottom by men from the Greenhithe yard prior to replating.

The Jubilee of King George V and Queen Mary on 6th May was an occasion for nationwide civic commemoration and at Riverside Gardens a street party was organised at which his worship the Mayor of Hammersmith attended and was photographed wearing with his chain of office. A Maypole bedecked with ribbons had been erected, the children of the estate sat at table, their mothers standing grouped around holding their youngest, and other residents looked out of their windows. Perhaps one of the mothers there was Ada with young June who was coming up to her first birthday.

The residents of Riverside Gardens were probably aware of the plans of the Borough of Hammersmith to change the character of their creekside area. Some time earlier, the Council had decided they needed a new Town Hall and had more or less settled on a site at Brook Green. However, some members thought that as the borough was a riparian authority it would be more appropriate for the Council to meet in a new Town Hall constructed overlooking the River Thames.

The Brewery had closed down and the Council had decided to demolish the old malthouse and other buildings fronting the creek and culvert the outfall of the Stamford Brook. To do this they had to fill in Hammersmith Creek and obtain the consent of the Port of London Authority to build a new river wall. This was duly forthcoming in principle and plans were prepared, but Julius Sax & Co. objected to the wall right across the mouth of the creek. So the Council went back to the P.L.A. with a proposal to build the wall at the site of the High Bridge. A month or so later the objectors were bought out and on 27th March 1935, the P.L.A. granted permission to straighten the river boundary and construct a new outlet in the wall to discharge the Stamford Brook sewer.

At the Chatham shipyard of Doust & Co. the work to *Prowess* continued to be noted in the logbook until Empire Day, 24th May, after which no further entries were made during her stay. On 5th July 1935, the skipper, George Douglas and Charles himself joined *Audacity* under her regular master, 46 year old naturalised Dutchman C.W. Wingfield, of Greenhithe. As the mate, Douglas was paid £4.6s.9d. a week and Charlie Fielder got £3.8s.3d. as second mate.

They sailed at 6 p.m. that evening deep laden for Schiedam, arriving at 11.30 a.m. the following morning, *Prowess* returned to Greenock empty to load for London on 16th, then sailed light ship to Aberdeen before returning to London on 23rd July where, on the 25th, the entire crew were discharged. Her Crew List shows that *Audacity* had been laid up since 7th June 1935, following passages to Zwijndrecht, Zaandam, Selby, Liverpool, Dover, Dundee, Hull, and Swansea but, on her return, undertook passages beyond the Home Trade Limits until 7th August, when she returned to Selby to resume trade to and from her usual ports of call.

When he was recalled to *Prowess* on 12th September, Charlie Fielder was the only one of the crew who had come from the *Audacity*. His new skipper was to be Capt. E. Liley, aged 37, from Gravesend, who had previously served in the *Authority*, a somewhat larger tanker of 616 grt. His crew included able seaman J. Woolstone, aged 58, from Gorleston who had come from the firm's former schooner *Capable* and the ordinary seaman G.A. Gibbon, aged 26, from Eastbourne. W.E. Cooper, aged 24, from Whitstable, was his chief engineer moving from the *Activity* while W.G. Gibbon, aged 32, was his Scottish number. two. The entry for the log was made when *Prowess* was lying off Greenhithe, having received orders to proceed to Knollendam to load linseed oil for Hull.

Engine trouble was reported during their return voyage in unfavourable weather conditions and on berthing at Seatons Wharf, a ship's boat was found to be damaged owing to stress of weather. On discharging the cargo it too, was found to be slightly damaged. It seems the main tank cover packing had worked, allowing sea water to enter No.4 tank. The south-west gale was still blowing with heavy squally rain when they finished discharging at 4 p.m. on Wednesday. *Prowess* went to a lay-by berth to await instructions from London and an inspection by a Lloyds surveyor, who recorded that 35 cwt. of cargo had been damaged and issued a Declaration Certificate to this effect.

Within a few years of Charlie's first visit aboard Prowess to Eagle Oil Mills in the Hull River, it was no more, a victim of German Luftwaffe bombing in May 1941.

Alchymist arrived on Friday with a shipment of cotton oil, 200 tons of which were for transshipment to Eagle Oil Mills. She was delayed in the river due to the breakdown of a windlass, but with assistance from a tug was able to get away for the 90 minute passage up to Eagle Oil Mills wharf to discharge. Orders were received to proceed to Yarmouth Roads but the Hull

River bridges were not worked on Sunday, so it was Monday 23rd September before *Prowess* was able to motor out of the harbour. She received orders by signal from Yarmouth Pier to proceed to Zaandam to load at Wormerveer.

After the some delays the ship returned to Hull to discharge her tanks and to turn round to head for the Hook of Holland and Zwijndrecht to load linseed oil at Jurgens Wharf on Wednesday 2nd October. After a day windbound she sailed to Leith, Scotland, where a Pilot brought her alongside the quay on Sunday 6th. The discharge of the cargo was completed on Tuesday afternoon, the compass adjusted and *Prowess* proceeded in the evening through rough seas to pass the Humber Light just after midnight. After an hour, about five miles from the inner Dowsing, the skipper decided to turn back to the Humber due to 'stress of weather'.

Underway on Friday evening, the engineer reported a defect at 6.50 p.m. so the engine was stopped to let him remedy the problem. After wallowing without power, the ship was underway again in an hour to arrive at Ijmuiden at 8.30 p.m. and moor temporarily at Zaandam at 10.15. Next day, Sunday 12th October, was spent in moving to the factory berth, discharging the ballast water and cleaning the tanks. The cargo of linseed oil loaded was for Rotherhithe where, on 16th, part of the consignment was transferred to the tank lighter *Outward*. Capt. Liley had had enough of the *Prowess* and on medical advice resigned his command to be replaced at short notice by B. Seaman of Wells who had previously commanded the little Wivenhoe built 144 grt, 89ft long, *Annuity*.

Leaving Younghusband's Wharf at 5pm on Thursday 17th October, *Prowess* arrived alongside Purfleet jetty to load gas oil for Portsmouth. The cargo was discharged on Saturday morning when the ship proceeded to Camber to moor alongside the steamer *Irishman*. The crew steam cleaned the main cargo tanks while lying weatherbound. On Sunday morning they continued on passage to Dieppe but anchored off Seaford to await a lull in the weather. It came and next day they crossed the Channel, picked up a Pilot to the Fish Dock to load linseed oil destined for Seaton's Wharf in Hull and a change of cargo.

Prowess was to revert to the Molasses trade which had become the mainstay of her carrying a few years previously, a trade for which she had been found well-suited, especially as the sugar beet refineries used steam in abundance, making it easily available to heat the cargo to enable pumping aboard. *Prowess* was a motor ship so, unlike her contemporaries, the firm's steam tankers *Alchymist*, *Agility* and *Audacity*, she was reliant on shore steam to both load and discharge her cargo.

Molasses is the residue of the sugar refining process, a sometimes golden, sometimes almost black, treacle like substance, largely carbohydrate, though still with 5% sugar content, but that too expensive and difficult to extract. It was sold to animal feed manufacturers in the U.K. and abroad for embodiment into cattle-feed pellets. Eventually it was realised that the sugar beet fibrous root waste itself would combine well with the molasses by-product and so animal feed pellets were, and still are, manufactured in-house at Cantley and other beet processing factories, signalling an end to the kind of molasses trade enjoyed by the *Prowess* in her day.

She made the passage from Hull to King's Lynn in ballast on Saturday, 26th October 1935, passing under the low bridge at Boal Quay to moor at the sugar beet factory at 10.30 a.m. next morning. During loading there were typical problems; a loading pipe burst and the shore pump stopped working but, by Monday evening the tanks were filled, dipped and measured, *Prowess* ready to leave. The Pilot came on board at 9.20 a.m. to take the ship through the bridge and moor to buoys to await the flood tide while her crew rigged the mast, derricks and deck gear. At 9 p.m. the Pilot was dropped at the Barr Flat Buoy and *Prowess* headed for Ipswich. It was a rough passage in a westerly gale and they had to anchor off Harwich to await the midnight tide to proceed to Cliff Quay. There the steaming coils were started and pumping begun to discharge the cargo.

At 12.30 next day, 1st November, they were on passage back to King's Lynn, mooring alongside the M.V. *Asperity* at noon on Saturday to unrig the deck gear. They moved up to the factory

In the shadows under the low railway bridge, *Prowess* just clears the ironwork, her mast lowered to avoid the girders, this close shave essential to save their tide at the factory wharf.

wharf to load, finishing at 11.20 p.m., for the return to Ipswich. Again they had to wait for the right time to pass under the bridge, then re-rig the deck gear and drop the Pilot.

Alongside Cliff Quay, steaming the molasses started at 10.15 a.m. but this time the cargo was very heavy and insufficiently liquid so the wharf manager gave instructions to stop pumping, but not before the coupling bolts broke, the pump stopped, and even when repaired they made slow progress owing to more trouble with the pump's gear box. In the end they had to rely on steam from a barge to complete the discharge at midnight.

Her mast still lowered, the crew aboard *Prowess* pose for the camera at King's Lynn. Left to right they are the Cook, the A.B., the 1st. Engineer, the 2nd. Engineer Vic Dines, the Mate Charlie Fielder and the Master.

They sailed for Greenhithe on the tide next morning. The yard engineers were aboard as soon as they arrived at 9 a.m. on the 7th to dismantle and rebuild the ship's pump. *Prowess* left on Saturday evening and after visiting the bunkering jetty reached King's Lynn ready to load on Monday morning. However there were further problems with coupling bolts, so that on 14th the Felixstowe Dock & Railway Company's steam tug had to be engaged to steam the cargo.

Distillery Wharf was one time London home of Haig whisky, before becoming the site of the Manbré & Garton sugar factory.

After discharging the cargo they were forced to anchor weatherbound in southerly gales before proceeding to Gt. Yarmouth and then to go up the river to Cantley to load. On Wednesday 20th November the laden *Prowess* arrived at Greenhithe for orders, picked up a waterman at 2.30 p.m. to proceed way up river to Distillery Wharf, just downstream of Charlie's flat at Hammersmith.

The ship berthed at 10.00 p.m. and the steam pipes were connected at 6.30 a.m. next morning, but before she could start to discharge they had to await Customs men who came aboard to dip and measure the tanks. At 11.30 a.m. the steam was supplied from the shore and the ship's pump began to discharge their molasses. Next morning started with an hour of steaming before discharge could restart at 10 a.m. and finish two hours later. At high water they had to move the ship to a temporary mooring on barge roads before getting underway down river to Greenhithe on passage for Gt. Yarmouth to await orders.

It was no surprise to be asked to proceed to Cantley again and, after a wait for the bridge to open, *Prowess* went up river to moor alongside the sugar beet factory. Finished loading on Monday morning, they set off for the Molasses Wharf of the Molasine Company of East Greenwich.

This Company had been founded in 1900 to exploit a secret formula for animal food, Molasine Meal. The recipe came from a mysterious east european, Arthur Stein, who vanished in Prague during the Second World War. The Greenwich factory in Tunnel Avenue opened in 1908 using molasses bought from local firms and the first steel tanks were installed there in 1910. The company's main product was a feed for horses made from sphagnum moss mixed with molasses and magnesium carbonate. During W.W.I this was used by soldiers as an antiseptic for wounds. The animal feed business in Greenwich was closed in 1981 when the machinery was transferred to Burton-on-Trent where the products continued to be made. The company had been taken over by Tate and Lyle some years previously and the site was put to use by other subsidiaries.

Steaming started at 2.10 p.m.; pumping an hour and twenty minutes later, continuing through the night into Thursday, but they were still having difficulty discharging the cargo. On Friday they had to bring in a shore pump to help the discharge, which was eventually completed enabling *Prowess* to get underway down river at 3.30 a.m. on Saturday 30th November for Gt. Yarmouth again, where they were to moor alongside overnight to wait, in gale force winds, for the bridge to open.

The molasses taken on board on Monday 2nd December, was again destined for Hammersmith. The ship's gear was lowered to go above the bridges to arrive off Distillery Wharf at 6.30 p.m. Moored alongside, the steamcocks were connected over Tuesday night. Discharging the cargo was, this visit, aided by three pumps supplied by the consignee and continued through the day and night finishing at 6 a.m. on Thursday. Next day they were underway down river at 12.20 p.m. After passing

Orfordness at 1.30 a.m. on Saturday speed was reduced in fog to proceed cautiously for Yarmouth and anchor off the pier at 11pm in a real 'pea-souper'. On Sunday 8th December they went through the bridge taking the sailing barge *Will Everard* in tow for Cantley to load on Monday.

Will Everard, last of Everard's big sailing coasters to grace these pages, but first to be built, going into service in July 1925. Sailing barges would be helped into Gt. Yarmouth by the harbour tugs, but would await a ship or up-river tug for the journey on to Cantley and beyond.

Prowess was away from the Cantley wharf on Tuesday with the S.B. *Greenhithe* in tow, clearing the bridge and, after casting off the barge, they moored alongside the town quay, her day's work done. *Prowess* was at Greenhithe overnight before leaving for Hammersmith, an hour later than hoped, owing to a starting gear defect on the main engine, She arrived at Distillery Wharf up above bridges at 2.30 p.m., Thursday 12th December, to berth alongside and start steaming the cargo. The discharge was completed at 11.45 a.m. next morning, after which they left Hammersmith with the crew rigging her mast and derricks to proceed straight back to Gt.

Yarmouth then Cantley. They moored just after noon outside the firm's M.V. *Acclivity* which was also waiting to load.

Loading completed, the tanks were dipped and the steam pipes disconnected, but owing to failing light, sailing was delayed until the morning of Wednesday 18th. They arrived off Hammersmith at 6.30 p.m. next day but were unable to berth alongside as there was insufficient water. Steam was sent through the coils at 4.40 p.m. for 20 minutes before starting to discharge through pipe lines laid across a barge. Discharging continued throughout the night so they were still pumping next morning before they could start to wash out the tanks in readiness for high water at 11 p.m. on Saturday. They did not float.

Greenhithe, forerunner of the big four Everard barges, awaits a tow at Gt. Yarmouth.

It was not until until 1 p.m. on Sunday that they were able to get away but soon ran into dense fog in Sea Reach and had to stay at anchor for the whole of Monday. There was a partial clearance at 1 a.m. when the master decided to get underway again. The firm's barges *Britisher* and *Greenhithe* were taken in tow from Yarmouth at 1.45 p.m. on Tuesday 24th and *Prowess* moored alongside at the Cantley sugar beet factory jetty at 6.30 p.m. on Christmas Eve.

Whether or not Charlie was able to get back to Ada and the family for Christmas is not clear but presumably they had already had some time together when the ship was beneaped just downstream of their home at Hammersmith Creek. Charlie's father was still working on the river as master of the sailing barge *Agnes Mary*, but although the official Crew List for the first half of 1935 has not survived, that for the second half year covering the period 1st July to 31st December, 1935 shows that his youngest son Wally, then aged 19, was mate with him. Ten years earlier *Agnes Mary* had been regularly working between Colchester, Gt. Yarmouth and Lowestoft in addition to carrying cement from Tunnel Works under her then master, Capt. R. Pringle of Chatham.

Loading *Prowess* commenced at 7 a.m. on Friday 27th and finished at 4 p.m. Next day she left Cantley at 8.30 a.m. with both *Alf Everard* and *Greenhithe* in tow but owing to bad weather they moored alongside Yarmouth Quay at 8 p.m., presumably after a look 'outside'. Sunday saw the ship underway at 8.30 again, passing the Yarmouth piers en-route to Vlaardingen Oil Wharf on the Nieuwe Maas, just downstream of Rotterdam. They arrived at 3 a.m. on Monday morning but had to wait five hours to connect to the shore pipes before commencing steaming around 9 a.m. which enabled discharging of the cargo at 10.50 a.m. The ship's onboard pump was disconnected in favour of those on shore, which continued until work ceased at 5 p.m. starting again next morning, the last day of 1935.

Wednesday 1st January 1936 was a national holiday in the Netherlands so *Prowess* lay at Vlaardingen Matex Wharf idle all day. Discharging the molasses was resumed at 6 a.m. on the 2nd and was finished at 2 p.m. when ballast water was pumped into the main tank. Due to an adverse weather report, departure was delayed until the morning. A Pilot came aboard at 6 a.m. and they proceeded on passage, dropping him at the Hook of Holland, and making for Gt. Yarmouth at full speed. *Prowess* passed the Maas Light at 9.50 a.m. and Gorleston Piers at 10.10 p.m. to moor alongside Yarmouth Quay at 10.45.

On Saturday the sailing barges *Veronica* and *Lady Maud* were taken in tow for Norwich but as it was dark at 4.30 p.m. they moored at the Cantley sugar beet wharf. The tow was continued on the Sunday, but they were overtaken by the firm's M.V. *Amenity* so the sailing barges were passed over to her for the rest of their voyage to Norwich. *Prowess* returned to Cantley but was unable to load on Monday as the management were waiting for M.V. *Acclivity* so *Prowess* had to move clear and did not start to load until midday on Tuesday. On Wednesday 8th

Everard's *Lady Maud* was built by them at Greenhithe, but to the order of Charles Charleton, adopting the Everard bob when purchased by the company in December 1915.

January *Prowess* moored outside the sailing barge *Britisher* to take on fresh water and her Master decided to wait for better weather next day, for the return passage to the Matex Oil Factory at Vlaardingen.

Despite delaying her departure, after passing out through Yarmouth Piers the southerly wind increased and developed into a full gale. The skipper decided to turn back after logging some 35 miles but in a heavy confused seas with the ship labouring in violent squalls it was just after midnight she passed between the piers into the harbour to moor alongside the Berry & Palmer Coal Quay.

The crew spent the next day making her shipshape pumping water from a fuel tank, but remaining weatherbound with no prospect of an abatement. 'Rather Cold' was noted on Sunday 12th when they were able to get underway to proceed to anchor in the River Maas just after midnight. A couple of hours later they were able to get alongside the factory to start to steam the tanks to heat the cargo. After three hours of steaming the molasses was ready to be discharged but it took three days to complete the job. At 1 a.m. on Thursday it was recorded that the crew were engaged in washing out the tanks. This was to be the last molasses for four months. The tanks were ballasted ready for the passage out passing the Hook of Holland at 6 a.m. to hug the coast to Ijmuiden for Zaandam to berth at Koog aan de Zaan.

Prowess loaded 200 tons of linseed oil, but northerly gales kept her alongside the canal bank until Sunday 18th, when she left for Seatons Wharf, Hull, arriving at 3.20 a.m. next day. The death of His Majesty King George V was reported at 11.56 p.m. on Tuesday 20th January 1936 and duly noted in the log. The oil discharge ran into a second day and the ship left Hull in ballast on Wednesday 21st January for the Erith Oil Works. There *Prowess* loaded cotton seed oil for Purfleet where it was discharged at Jurgens' factory. Back to Erith again, this time for

180 tons of peanut oil, but the discharge of the cargo was delayed while Everard's S.S. *Alchymist* discharged first. Back at Greenhithe the crew set about washing the tanks through for the next cargo.

On Monday 27th January *Prowess* left to cross the river to Anglo's Caspian Jetty. The tanks were rejected by the surveying inspector so she had to go back to Greenhithe alongside the steam tug *Faverolle* to steam clean them. After

an hour steaming each tank the crew had to rewash and dry them. At 7.30 p.m. they had finished with the tanks for the day and moved from the upper to the middle buoy off the yard. Next day, Tuesday 28th January was a National Day of Mourning for the late King George V, so while the crew spent more time cleaning the tanks, the order to load lubricating and spindle oils was deferred until the following day. The cargo was for Anglo's Wharf on the River Hull and was duly discharged, save for 50 tons which were for Seatons Wharf, where the *Prowess* went with help from the steam tug *Rover*. The last of the cargo was emptied on Saturday 1st February and the ship returned to Purfleet to repeat the freight, before returning to Yarmouth Roads for orders.

Saturday 8th February saw *Prowess* at anchor under the lee of Scroby Sands off Gt.Yarmouth safe from an easterly gale with 45 fathoms cable out. It was not until 4 p.m. on Tuesday that they attempted to put a small boat ashore but it returned to the ship to report that it was too rough to land and was hoist back aboard. At five they got underway for Zaandam with the moderating gale then from the south-east. They were directed to Knollendam where their berth was occupied by the M.V. *Helena* but by nightfall they had loaded 200 tons of linseed oil. They sailed for Gravesend with their pratique[1] and orders to deliver the cargo overside into lighters at Younghusband, Barnes & Company's Wharf. However, they were delayed by the non-arrival of an extra barge to complete the discharge, as a consequence of which the ship took the ground and they were unable to sail on the Saturday tide.

Next day orders were received to sail to Southampton, but dense fog prevented their departure. The fog lifted during Monday morning and they started their passage passing Beachy Head in the early hours of Tuesday, where they ballasted the ship in the light of a strong south-westerly gale. Midday saw them at anchor off Netley Hospital, in Southampton Water. When the tide served at 4.30 p.m. *Prowess* weighed anchor for Northam on the River Itchen, where linseed oil was loaded during Wednesday, before sailing next day. The oil was destined for the Greenwich Inlaid Linoleum Works and discharged there on Saturday 22nd. Then it was back to Zaandam for more oil. This was for Younghusband's and discharged there on 4th March into the tank barges *Forward* and *Classic*. That job done, the ship returned to Greenhithe buoys to moor alongside the sailing barge *Martha* for engine room repairs, whilst the crew turned their attention to the routine cleaning of the cargo tanks, working on them through the night and next day.

The next trip was from Anglo's Purfleet Jetty with oil for their Newcastle upon Tyne depot, *Prowess* departing at 3 p.m. on Friday 6th March. The ship was off Flambro' Head at 11 p.m. on Saturday logging 107 miles, taking on the Tyne Pilot at 9.40 on Sunday morning to wait for the tide off South Shields until 3.45 p.m., before the half-hour run up to Anglo's Wharf. Using the ship's own pump the cargo was discharged by 3.30 p.m. on Monday. A Pilot was taken

[1] Clearance granted to a ship to proceed into port after compliance with health regulations or quarantine.

111

The steam tug *King Edward VII* had moved north to the Tyne from Gt. Yarmouth.

The Kattendijk Locks were a busy place; liners, sailing craft and continental waterway barges all queuing for the locks, a new destination for Everard's *Prowess*.

aboard to proceed down river, with orders for Belgium, to tie alongside the ex. Gt. Yarmouth steam paddle tug *King Edward VII* on buoys to pump ballast and await favourable weather. *Prowess* left for sea just before midday next morning in dense fog. At midnight, on a course S.S.E., the log had recorded 91.3 miles. At 8.30 a.m. next morning, she had logged 159 miles with the Foulness buoy abeam; 171 miles on the log found her at the Cockle lightvessel, after which she ran into fog off the Corton Light at 12.15 p.m.

It was some twelve hours later before she arrived off De Heen Banks, sighting a Pilot cutter before arriving at Kattendijk Locks to moor alongside barges to await Customs clearance. The crew had to unship the mast and derricks to proceed to Antwerp where *Prowess* commenced loading linseed oil at 2 p.m. on Friday 13th March. Pumping finished at 10.40 p.m. recording the draught at 8.0 feet forward and 8.7 feet aft and the tonnage 219. On Saturday she was underway from the canal to the locks dropping the Pilot at Vlissingen, where the sea Pilot came aboard. He left the ship at midnight and they proceeded to Younghusband's Wharf arriving at 5.25 p.m. on a rather cold Sunday March evening. The oil was discharged next morning to

the barge *Leeward* and *Classic* while the crew repainted *Prowess's* Plimsoll marks before the regular chore of tank cleaning, washing and drying.

Prowess loaded batching oil at Purfleet on Thursday 19th March for Dundee, where she arrived at 6.55 p.m. on Saturday 21st to await the midnight tide and enter the docks to discharge and await the arrival of a new engineer. The weather deteriorated, the crew spending their time painting until 2 p.m. when a better weather forecast was received and they sailed with the Pilot on board. He was dropped at the Tay Bar Buoy where the course was set south-south-east. At the Abbs Head Light they encountered dense fog but continued on course in a heavy swell sounding the depth by the lead and making continuous sound signals. The fog continued next morning and with seas becoming rougher the master decided to anchor in Yarmouth Roads, the crew having been on duty for 18 hours.

Conditions improved overnight so at 10.10 a.m. *Prowess* got underway for Zaandam only to run into more dense fog as they approached the Dutch coast. Leadline soundings were taken until at 11.55 they anchored in 5½ fathoms near the coast, with anchor watches being kept. Engine problems on Saturday morning delayed their start but at 8.10 a.m. a Pilot came onboard to take them through the locks at Zaandam Sluis. On arrival at Hartz Fabriek the loading of 200 tons of linseed oil commenced while further engine repairs were carried out. These did not stop the ship getting underway at 7.30 a.m. for Ijmuiden to clear the locks for London. Their pratique was received in Gravesend Reach at 1.20 p.m., a seaman transferred at Greenhithe, before mooring at Rotherhithe to prepare for unloading on Tuesday 31st March.

Further adverse weather delayed the next load of lubricating oils for Hull, forcing the skipper to turn back to anchor off the Scroby Sands. It was Saturday 4th April before *Prowess* came to anchor in Hull Roads in the early hours, there to await sufficient water at Anglo's wharf to discharge part of her cargo before proceeding upriver to Seatons. Sunday was spent washing, cleaning and drying the tanks to be ready to move to Stonesferry Oil Mills to load 220 tons of cotton oil for transshipment to the S.S. *Lochkatrine* in London. Continuing engine repairs delayed the ship until the next morning's tide when *Prowess* was joined by the firm's S.S. *Alchymist* at the Old Harbour entrance for the passage to the Royal Albert Dock. The ship arrived alongside the *Lochkatrine* to start to discharge at 7.25 p.m. with steam being supplied by *Alchymist*. The log records that the discharge finished at 2.10 a.m. in the morning of Thursday 9th April with the ship leaving the King George V Dock entrance for Caspian Jetty at Purfleet to load 200 tons of gas oil for Portsmouth.

More bad weather made *Prowess* anchor off Southend. She had to stop again next morning owing to a problem with the main engine. The engineers worked throughout the day, the log reporting that the cylinder head had cracked and the starting gear was out of order. Nevertheless they were under way by 7.45 p.m. passing the Nore and Girdler lights overnight. Dungeness was passed around breakfast time and by dinner time Saturday 11th April, the anchor was dropped off Spithead.

Within the jurisdiction of the Portsmouth Royal Navy base and the King's Harbour Master, a cargo certificate signed by the Collector of Customs at the port of loading, declaring the oil free of vapour at below 75° F., would have to be provided and the Harbour Master's permission would have been needed for *Prowess* to moor at Flathouse Quay, in Fountain Lake on the Portsmouth shore close to the gasworks, to discharge her cargo. Unloaded by just before 5.00 p.m., *Prowess* proceeded to Netley where the steam tug *Beaulieu* supplied steam to clean the tanks. They were under way to the Solent at 11 a.m. next morning to moor at Messrs. Cardew & Dixon, Northam, to load unrefined cotton oil, taking all day Tuesday. The ship left for London at 4.30 a.m. on Wednesday to moor at Greenhithe at 6.10 a.m. the following morning.

Fifty tons were discharged into a barge but, with the weather being rather cold, the firm's steam tug *Faverolle* was ordered to steam the cargo at midnight before *Prowess* left for Owen Parry's wharf, Millwall. She got no further than Gallions Reach before her Newbury main engine broke down and the crew had to get a line onto the buoys at 9.40 a.m. The tug arrived to take the ship in tow just after eight o'clock that evening, but when they arrived at the wharf there was insufficient water, so the tug had to remain in attendance all night to put *Prowess* alongside and steam the cargo. At 11 p.m. *Faverolle*, with *Prowess* in tow, was underway for Greenhithe buoys where the tanks were cleaned and, whilst the deck officer's log makes no mention of mechanical matters, presumably the engineers were then able to remedy the engine issues.

Certainly there is no mention of the engine in the log for the next three freights of gas oil from Anglo's Caspian Jetty, Purfleet, for the Bournemouth & Poole Gas Works, Dorset. There is some mention of rough seas and fog but the weather was generally fair with no untoward incidents. The handwriting indicates that Charlie Fielder did not himself write up the log for the last week of April.

The gas works on Poole Quay served Poole and nearby Bournemouth. The coal gantries predominate, with the gas oil tanks at the rear right of the coal heaps.

Indeed the log shows that after receiving orders at Greenhithe on Monday 4th May Charlie Fielder was relieved from duty for an indefinite period owing to ill health. The loading was supervised by the mate of M.V. *Ramble* which, like the firm's *Saunter, Roam, Wander, Frank Pink* and *Stanley Baldwin*, was a former Admiralty dry cargo lighter, completed in 1915. All bar *Frank Pink* and *Stanley Baldwin* were converted to tankers.

Charlie was away sick for a fortnight, but for Monday 11th May the diary has a retrospective note in his hand 'this ship on this day reported to have struck submerged wreckage 15 miles S.E. x S. from Longstone Light, no damage apparent, Longstone Lt. bearing N.W. x W.' The following day the ship arrived ready for discharging but it was discovered that 'The cargo in Nos. 3 - 4 tanks had been damaged by sea water entering by valve on deck. Tanks 1 and 2 being discharged the remainder being freighted back to London'.

The entry for Friday 15th May, 1936 states 'Arrival at Purfleet and discharged damaged cargo and then ordered to shipyard for inspecting and survey and also minor repairs, myself returning from sick leave to return for duty on this day.'. Clearly, whatever prompted the 'indefinite period' of sick leave was not to endure for long.

Charlie's first passage back aboard was in ballast from Greenhithe to Southampton on Saturday 16th May. Before getting underway from the yard another engine defect was reported so the ship stopped on the buoys until 10 p.m. The weather being fine and warm they had an easy trip and arrived at 8.10 p.m. on Sunday before starting to load linseed oil on Monday. Loading was finished at midnight, ready to sail for London in a light westerly wind. By Wednesday evening, off the South Foreland, the wind swung round to a strong north-easterly with very rough seas, the ship labouring and making slow progress. These conditions continued all the way up the Thames until their arrival off Greenwich at the Inlaid Linoleum Works Jetty, where *Prowess* moored alongside at 11.35 a.m. and started to discharge to shore tanks shortly after midday, finishing at 11.15 p.m. that night.

Next day, Friday 22nd May, the crew cast off from the Greenwich jetty at 3.30 a.m. for Greenhithe buoys. Whilst alongside the barge roads for a couple of hours the crew had time to wash and dry the tanks before proceeding to Purfleet to load lubricating oil for Hull. This delivered, they had another rough and unpleasant passage in ballast to Holland for 170 tons of linseed oil, returning on Saturday 30th May to Greenhithe for orders to proceed to Younghusband's Wharf, Rotherhithe for the Whitsun holiday. The pipelines were connected on Tuesday morning but the coupling bolts on the pump gear broke and pumping was suspended for the day while the engineers carried out repairs.

Back at Greenhithe, the 3rd of June brought news of the start of the 1936 sugar beet 'Campaign' with orders for Cantley, returning to the Molasine Wharf, before bunkering at

Sailing barges gather at the Cantley sugar factory. Some may load at Cantley, but the river tug, right, will tow others to Norwich.

Purfleet. Back again to Cantley for a further cargo of molasses, but on the third successive run, on Friday 26th June, the main engine gave further problems. Forced to anchor two miles from the N.E. Gunfleet buoy, the ship's engineer eventually got the engine running again on three cylinders, but the master decided to put into Harwich to telephone a report to the owners.

A maintenance engineer[2] was sent up from London, arriving late afternoon and four hours later, following a test run around the harbour, reported that the ship was ready to go, On Sunday morning they were under way at 5.45 a.m. on passage to Gt. Yarmouth, where they were again dogged by more engine trouble, though it did not stop them from arriving at Cantley next morning to load molasses for Greenwich.

Discharging this cargo ran into Thursday 2nd July, when the pump failed. An important component, the crosshead arm driving rod, had broken so they were ordered back to Greenhithe for repairs. The yard put things right, the crew washed the tanks and the *Prowess* set off back to Cantley taking the S.B. *Mary Graham* in tow. After loading they towed the sailorman back out to sea, bound for the London

[2.] The firm had a service engineer, Edgar Wildsmith, who rushed around the country on a motorcycle, to deal with engine problems large and small. He had an encyclopaedic knowledge of every engine in the fleet.

117

Deep laden, the firm's *Mary Graham* awaits a tow alongside Jewson's Wharf at Gt. Yarmouth.

River to deliver their cargo to the Molasine Wharf, East Greenwich. They picked up spare pump parts at Greenhithe, in case they were needed, although the pump worked throughout the night without problems. On 16th July the ship returned to Greenhithe for orders.

Prowess was diverted briefly from the sugar beet trade to take lubricating oil from the Anglo-American Purfleet wharf to Hull on 22nd July. A main engine stoppage on 22nd was caused by a burst fuel pipe but it only took half an hour to remedy. On this occasion Charlie noted that the wharf was now renamed the Esso Wharf. Returning to Greenhithe the ship was loaded with gas oil and ordered to Lowestoft to discharge at the Oulton Broad Depot.

From there it was straight to nearby Cantley to load molasses and take the S.B. *Veronica* in tow for Gt. Yarmouth where they left her on Saturday 1st August, before heading again for the Molasine Wharf, to arrive in time for the August Bank Holiday. On Tuesday the steam pipes were connected but, after an hour or so, the main shore pumps broke down and discharging was suspended. *Prowess* was told to lay off afloat on the barge moorings while the firm sent a pump from Greenhithe to get the discharge going again alongside the wharf, finishing midday on Friday 7th. The pump was dropped off at Greenhithe on the way down river and she continued on to Gt. Yarmouth, then Cantley, but no work was started at the sugar jetty, as it was a half-day holiday.

It is hard to imagine the sailing barge *Veronica* as a cargo carrying workhorse of the coastal trade, when seen here 25 years later competing in the annual Thames Sailing Barge Match, completing the 48 mile course at an astonishing average speed of almost 12 knots.

It was not until Friday 14th August that loading was completed but, at Wenn's Wharf, while waiting for the bridge, they encountered more minor engine trouble. Despite this, *Prowess* carried on out past the piers and back up to the Thames. At Greenhithe they took a steaming pump on board and went on up to Greenwich, where they were able to start discharging at the Molasine Wharf on Monday morning. Unloading took all day and all night until 2.45 p.m. on Tuesday, but even then some cargo remained in the tanks. However, on 16th August they had orders to return to Greenhithe to lay alongside the *Alchymist* and wash out their tanks in readiness for a change in cargo.

The next freight was linseed oil from Knollendam Fabriek, Wormerveer. *Prowess* left Greenhithe on 18th August being turned round in Holland within a day to berth alongside Seatons Wharf, Hull, on Saturday 22nd August. Discharging took all day on Monday but they were alongside a hopper barge in Dieppe by Midnight on Wednesday 26th August. More linseed oil was loaded on 28th for delivery at Rotherhithe followed by another cargo for Seatons, where they had to wait for *Acclivity* to discharge before going alongside on Saturday 5th September.

Discharging was extended over four days before another four day round trip with more for Seatons. Orders for East Halton followed and *Prowess* anchored in White Booth Roads so that the master could inspect the berth in daylight. The crew were left cleaning and drying the tanks while the skipper went ashore and discovered that the remote berth was very muddied, but he was ordered from London to attempt to berth on the afternoon. The ship went alongside the steep-to causeway berth at 6.50 p.m. Tuesday 15th, the weight of the *Prowess* putting a heavy strain on the mooring wires when the tide went away. Next morning an Inspector from London passed the tanks and they started to load a superfine lubricating oil which took about eight hours.

At 11 p.m., as the ebb was leaving her, some of the ship's moorings carried away leaving only the head ropes and wires attached to the shore. *Prowess's* stern slid down the slope and over the causeway. The crew had spent all night standing by to move ship and anchor in the channel on the flood tide. At 3 a.m. on the flood tide *Prowess* floated without any apparent damage, but beforehand it was seen that the causeway had not fared so well. They proceeded to clear the causeway and anchor in the channel. Two hours later the anchor was retrieved and *Prowess* proceeded on passage to London. At 7.30 a.m. on Friday 18th main engine trouble was reported and they stopped at anchor in dense fog. By 10.45 the engine was considered satisfactory, so they proceeded on passage for lubricating oil suppliers W. B. Dick & Co. Ltd.'s Pageant's Wharf, Rotherhithe. The ship was alongside at 11.45 p.m. and discharged the cargo next day to return to bunker at Purfleet and on to Greenhithe for orders.

On Monday 21st September the ship's Master received orders for

The Royal Warrant on this lubricants advertisement from a 1930s Punch magazine, suggests *Prowess's* cargo may well have been royal oil!

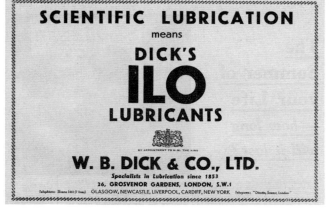

SCIENTIFIC LUBRICATION
means
DICK'S
ILO
LUBRICANTS

W. B. DICK & CO., LTD.
Specialists in Lubrication since 1853
26, GROSVENOR GARDENS, LONDON, S.W.1
GLASGOW, NEWCASTLE, LIVERPOOL, CARDIFF, NEW YORK

All along the Zaan were oil mills; here at Koog aan de Zaan on the west bank, to the left of the Mallegatsluis, is an oil mill with storage tank and piles of oil barrels line the quay to the right.

Oughtred & Harrison's five-story warehouse and wharf fronting the River Hull. They were Everard's Humber area agent until c.1980.

Zaandam to load just 105 tons at Koog aan de Zaan for Hull. This was discharged at Seatons on 28th then, after minor engine problems, it was via Yarmouth Roads to Ijmuiden on 1st October. Water contamination in the fuel caused trouble in the main engine whilst delivering the next load of linseed oil for Rotherhithe. Again, on the following crossing, *Prowess's* engine stopped twice with water in the fuel but they entered Ijmuiden at midnight on 7th October.

Back at Rotherhithe they could not discharge until Monday as there was insufficient tank capacity ashore. There was a 'slight fire' from the main exhaust pipe which was quickly extinguished but, on their next visit to Zaandam *Prowess* was dogged by more main engine trouble and they were forced to anchor in the North Sea Canal to sort it out. This time a blockage in a fuel pipe was to blame. They reached their destination and loaded, before dipping the tanks. In failing light and adverse weather, a strong S.E. gale, they left the berth but were weatherbound in the Old South Canal until conditions improved. It wasn't until Thursday 22nd that *Prowess* was able to sail for Hull, where they had to anchor off to await a berth at Oughtred & Harrison's Wharf.

Some slight damage occurred to the fo'c'sle head and the rails when *Prowess* skewed off the berth, pulling a fairlead adrift on the port side. They moved to Seatons to discharge and left on 28th October

121

for Gt. Yarmouth where orders were received to return to Ijmuiden to load more linseed oil at various wharves there. They got under way, locking out to sea midday on Friday 6th November after a delay of two hours due to yet more engine trouble. At midnight in a southerly gale the Master decided to go for shelter with the sea confused and very rough. A Pilot came aboard off the Hook of Holland and directed the ship up river to anchor two miles above Maashaven, Rotterdam. Even within these sheltered waters they let go a second anchor to prevent dragging in the heavy squalls and were unable to land for stores on Monday, although next day they managed to get a small boat ashore.

During a lull *Prowess* got away down river as far as the Hook when a heavy thunderstorm and increasing wind drove them back up river to anchor. On Wednesday they were able to pick up radio reports from England of very bad weather there, with the barometer low and no sign of the local weather moderating. At last, on Friday 13th, they were able to get under way, proceeding on passage for London, passing out of the Hook at 8.30 p.m. the log reporting rain squalls, very cold weather and seas rough. On Saturday they passed the Nore Light at 6.50 a.m., receiving their Pratique at Gravesend, with orders at Greenhithe to go alongside Younghusband's Wharf, Rotherhithe, where *Prowess* arrived at 1 p.m. that day, Saturday 14th November 1936.

There was more trouble with *Prowess's* main engine and pumps; several delaying stoppages which meant that her cargo was not emptied until late on Tuesday. At 3 a.m. on Wednesday morning they cleared the berth for the arrival of the firm's S.S. *Alchymist* and were ordered alongside at Greenhithe, with the assistance of a motorboat, for repairs by the yard engineers and shipwrights.

Engine reliability could have a big impact on operational efficiency, with an inevitable knock-on effect on customer satisfaction. Although *Prowess*, a relatively new ship with just a decade of service in her log, seems to have suffered her share of engine room and machinery issues, she had been lucky so far to have lost very little time over repairs, most being sorted by her own crew; only very few needing the attention of her owner's shipyard. Add to this the fact that the Everard fleet had adopted Newbury engines from Plenty & Son Ltd. as preferred policy for new-build ships and replacements in second-hand tonnage from the early 1920s, and its ownership of the engine builder itself from 1932 cemented this commitment which was to endure for around forty years. There was therefore little competition with rival firms for spare parts and the familiarity with a single engine make must have had a positive impact on repair times.

It was in the mid-1930s that the new 'F' Type Newbury engine was introduced, around the same time as Everard had taken control of the Berkshire company. The 4 cylinder version illustrated was ultimately to replace the unreliable and earlier P50 type aboard *Prowess*.

Prowess left for Zaandam at 4 p.m. on Thursday 19th November to anchor a mile north-west of the Southend jetty, weatherbound and taking on water ballast. The ship lay there on Friday with no sign of the weather abating but got under way on Saturday to load linseed oil from a local barge at Zaandam and return on Tuesday afternoon to Greenhithe to await orders. On Thursday they were sent to Rotherhithe to discharge into the dumb barge *Leeward*.

Fresh orders for Zaandam's Koog aan de Zaan wharves saw *Prowess* back there by 9.15 p.m. on Saturday 21st. This part of the Netherlands became colloquially known as 'Zaanstreek' (Zaan = River Zaan; streek = region). With the Dutch tradition of dairy product manufacture, it is unsurprising that Zaanstreek became the centre for a huge diversity of foodstuff manufacturing and processing, not only in fats and edible oils, but where, for example, more than 20% of the world's cocoa bean crop was processed.

More winter gales led to the ship being weatherbound until Wednesday 9th December when she passed Ijmuiden pier en route to Rotherhithe where they commenced discharging on Thursday afternoon. From there *Prowess* motored to Purfleet for bunkers, Greenhithe for orders and then back to Zaandam for more linseed oil. Another strong gale at Ijmuiden left the ship weatherbound again, until the weather eased four days before Christmas, only for the crew to find the main engine stopped with water in the fuel. Nevertheless, they entered the sea locks at 9.30 a.m. and were at last under way back to the Humber. After logging 105 miles on a course north-west by north, the main engine died at 5.25 a.m. with water in the fuel supply again. After bleeding the fuel lines and clearing the filters the engine was restarted at 7.10 a.m. and the rest of the passage was completed without interruption. *Prowess* arrived alongside Seatons Wharf, Hull, with a tug in attendance, at 12.35 a.m. on Wednesday 23rd December, where discharge of her cargo was started straight away

Prowess's skipper decided to sail as soon as possible, Christmas Day, and by midnight they were off Blakeney in light, variable winds with 50.8 miles on the log. It had been rather mild during the day but cold at night. At 6.30 a.m. on Boxing Day morning the main engine stopped for half an hour, due to water in the fuel again. Dense fog closed in off the Dutch coast and they dropped anchor in just under six fathoms with anchor watches being kept. They were able to get under way at 8.00 a.m. to pick up a Pilot to take them into the North Sea Canal. *Prowess* moored alongside the bank to hear the big end of her Newbury engine making itself known, a much more serious problem than water contaminated fuel. Cautiously they were able to make their way through the entrance lock next morning to moor up to await the barge that was bringing their cargo of linseed oil.

After loading they remained to allow engineers to examine the main bearing and effect at least a temporary fix to get *Prowess* home. Water in the fuel stopped the engine again at 2 p.m. and when it died again at 9.30 the trouble seemed to be a leaking head joint, possibly allowing cooling water into the engine valves or cylinders. The repair efforts seemed to have worked, for by Thursday 31st December 1936 *Prowess* had arrived at Younghusband's Wharf, after a slight impact with barges on Bellamy's Roads, with no apparent damage done, to start discharging next morning.

Charlie Fielder's diary for 1937 starts with a memorandum entitled 'Signing on of Crew Conditions' which follow - 'The crew shall work all cargos when and where required and shall give 24 hours notice of intention to leave and vice versa and shall not leave ship in any weatherbound or in [sic] foreign ports.' Perhaps of greater interest to Charlie, he has noted 'January 2nd 1937. Received raise of six shillings per cargo from 30th of November,

1936.' followed by a note of tons to kilos conversion '200 tons in Kilos 203.000' [Approximate conversion rate for Long Tons or U.K. tons to Kilos].

On Friday 1st January 1937 a Lloyds surveyor had come aboard to inspect the ships structure while the crew started discharging her cargo. This work continued during Saturday morning and it was 3.20 p.m. before they left Rotherhithe for Greenhithe to take on ship's stores. *Prowess* left on passage to Antwerp in a strong wind

Though aerial photography appears to flatten the seas, it is clear that a lively chop faces *Prowess* en-route to her next destination.

and rough sea. They picked up a Belgian sea Pilot who handed over to a river Pilot off Flushing, to make their way to their berth. There they were to load from a local motorbarge.

Monday was bright and sunny and loading the linseed oil was completed in four hours, but they had to wait until 4.30 p.m. to work down the dock to the lock, with the river Pilot back on board. By 11.30 p.m. the Master decided to go for the anchorage off Breskens owing to stress of weather. A wind shift exposed the Breskens Roads so they hove up the anchor to make for a safer anchorage off Hoe Gat. However, in the morning the anchor had dragged so the skipper decided to get underway and closer to the main channel where they gave her 30 fathoms of chain. The strong wind continued to blow. They were still weatherbound for all of the next day but at 9.15 a.m. on Friday 8th January *Prowess* got underway for London, receiving orders from Gravesend to berth at Rotherhithe to discharge on Monday.

Emptied same day, the ship moved to Purfleet for bunkering and Greenhithe for stores on Tuesday with orders to return to Antwerp, a slow and foggy passage. The return, bound for Younghusband's Wharf, was much easier, save for an hour at anchor in the estuary to repair, yet again, the main engine but, while unloading, the auxiliary engine stopped due to a cylinder head defect. The ship's engineers were unable to keep it running so they had to call for a shore pump to discharge the cargo, while the crew spent time overside painting the boot topping. On 20th January, with the oil discharged they left for Greenhithe, mooring to a buoy where the shore based engineers came aboard and worked on the auxiliary engine.

Next day *Prowess* left for Flushing and the Schelde River but on Sunday morning the main engine stopped. The ship anchored so that the engineer could work throughout the day, eventually tracing the problem to the recently repaired big ends. Eventually he managed to get the engine running on three of its four cylinders and they made their way in the very cold, strong, easterly wind and heavy rain to the Kattendijk Lock in Antwerp where they awaited customs clearance and contacted the Greenhithe yard. The mast and derricks had to

1930s Antwerp was a city reliant on waterborne trade, this postcard of the period showing the quayside crammed with ferries and other shipping.

be lowered before they got underway to moor alongside to load another cargo of linseed oil.

This took seven hours, after which they moved to a lay-by berth to await the engine bearing to arrive next day from England. While the crew took the opportunity to replace wire ropes and tarpaulins, the ship's engineers finished their repair and got the engine running, but were unable to try the propeller in gear for fear of excessive wash causing problems for other craft. At 9.15 a.m. on Wednesday 27th they were underway down the canal but within an hour collided with a locally owned motor vessel with slight damage to her port bow, but no apparent damage to the stern of the *Prowess*.

Locking out into the Shelde River they made their way down but found severe conditions and anchored weatherbound from Wednesday night until Saturday morning. Just two hours underway confirmed that conditions further down the estuary were still poor so *Prowess* came alongside a dutch motor vessel to await an improvement. Eventually conditions allowed the ship to proceed for Hull to discharge and take on soya bean oil for Greenhithe, where a full overhaul of the main engine was to be carried out.

Prowess berthed on Friday 5th February and remained at Greenhithe while the shore engineers worked on the main engine. There was heavy rain all day on the Sunday and a very cold night. It was decided to berth *Prowess* in the inner dock alongside the *Ramble* but there was insufficient width for the two ships abreast so she laid alongside *Apricity*. The ship was still under repair on Tuesday with the main cylinders being taken ashore.

Next day Charlie received orders go by motor boat to Purfleet to assist with loading barges. With lighterman H. Mills, he boarded the boat which was driven by Walter Collins. Whilst getting from the motor boat onto a barge Charlie Fielder was squeezed between the wheelhouse of the boat and the side of a barge, due to excessive wash from a tug proceeding up river at speed, causing the barge and boat to roll together. Concern over the extent of his injuries led to Charlie being taken back to Greenhithe where the firm's doctor ordered him home to bed.

The diary remains without entries for the remainder of the month, until Monday 1st March 1937 when Charlie Fielder returned to work. His eighteen days off as a result of the accident had allowed, what turned out to be a hip injury, sufficient time to recover. The 'recovery' of *Prowess* was to take longer, so on Thursday 4th he had orders to take charge of the firm's sailing barge *Her Majesty* and sail her in the river cement work until her skipper returned to duty. After less than a week in her, on Wednesday 10th March he arrived at Tunnel Works to load and later in the day was relieved by her regular master, so returned to Greenhithe and his own ship.

Prowess's main engine was ready for trials on the morning of Friday 12th March, and the crew of the firm's M.V. *Aqueity* came on board to assist Charlie. After running the main engine while stationary, Capt. A. Hadlow, who had twice commanded the steamer *Tosca*

whilst Charlie served in her, came aboard to take charge of the trials underway, returning to the mooring shortly after midday.

Three hours later they were underway for bunkers at Purfleet before going back down-

Fellows at Gt. Yarmouth had already built half a dozen motor ships for Everard by the time the dry cargo coaster *Aqueity* joined the Everard fleet in 1933.

river to Greenhithe. Next day, with Capt. Hadlow in command, *Prowess* left Greenhithe on passage to Zaandam to arrive off Ijmuiden piers and take on the Pilot. She locked in and moored alongside the Ferry Jetty at 7 p.m. on Passion Sunday. On Monday morning a Pilot came aboard to take the ship to Knollendam where *Prowess* moored alongside to commence loading. With 145 tons of linseed oil aboard they moved at noon to Wormerveer go load a further 70 tons and then moored alongside the canal bank in heavy rain and a north-west gale.

On Monday 15th March, 1937 there was a minor collision in the River Zaan. Charlie's diary has a note: 'While proceeding down river towards Zaandam on passage to London had minor collision with motor canal barge, name unknown, alongside quayside off Wormerveer, no apparent damage to our ship but damaged barge's bulwark and rails, caused by our anchor overhanging rails. Ship [*Prowess*], while approaching Wormerveer Bridge, had to stop owing to bridge not being opened and ship seemed to touch the ground with her keel aft and gale of wind N.W. ship became temporarily unmanageable so causing collision.'

Being windbound, the crew were working about the deck on various jobs, cleaning the wheelhouse brasswork, ports and compass binnacle cover, before at 8.10 p.m. on Wednesday 17th Capt. Hadlow decided that the weather had moderated sufficiently to go. *Prowess* got underway, locked out at Ijmuiden into the North Sea, arriving off Gravesend at 1.50 a.m. on Friday 19th March where she received her pratique. She carried on to Greenhithe, where her boat was sent ashore for orders. *Prowess* was to remain where she was pending the S.S. *Alchymist* clearing the discharge berth once unloaded. Capt. Hadlow received orders to rejoin his own ship, the steam tanker *Tartary*. This command was destined to be short-lived, as on 14th February 1938 she ran aground on the Haisborough Sands in bad weather when on passage from Zaandam to Hull with linseed oil. Although she was refloated, she foundered off Winterton and then exploded when cold sea water entered the boilers which still had a full head of steam.

With the departure of Capt. Hadlow, Charlie Fielder received orders to proceed to Rotherhithe and was given the assistance of a lighterman, W. Collins, to make up the numbers for the passage. They had to wait for the tide before mooring alongside Younghusband's Wharf, the discharge to be started on Monday, However there was no room in the shore tanks for the cargo, so that they had to wait until 5.50 p.m. to start but, just a couple of hours later the shore tanks were full. Next day the barge *Morningwatch* arrived to enable the discharge to be restarted, continuing until 2.00 p.m. by which time the tide had gone, causing the discharge to cease. So with the ship under the mate's command, Charlie had to wait for the next tide and with it the news he had perhaps anticipated and hoped for.

Charlie Fielder wrote in his log for Tuesday, 23rd March, 1937 'Myself appointed Master on this day of M.V. *Prowess*.' The morning had started with the crew resuming the discharge to the barge *Morning Watch*, a task completed in the early afternoon but not in time, the log records, to get off the berth before *Prowess* took the ground.

At 10.00 p.m., with the ship formally under his command, Capt. Charlie Fielder was underway down river for Greenhithe, arriving just after midnight for orders. At 1.00 p.m. next day the *Prowess* left for Zaandam, but ninety minutes later Capt. Fielder was forced to anchor in Sea Reach and recorded 'Main engine defective - cause oiling ring burnt out and stoppage of oil to bearings.' Nine hours later he was able to order the restarting of the engine and proceed outward with the weather worsening, the north westerly wind increasing and the visibility deteriorating as it got 'rather cold', according to the log. They berthed at Knollendam at 12.30 p.m. on Thursday and loaded 215 tons of linseed oil in five hours. Returning to Ijmuiden to exit the canal, the ship was forced to moor on the bank owing to 'stress of weather'. It was not until Sunday 28th March that they were able to get underway, arriving back at Greenhithe on the Easter Bank Holiday, before being sent on up to Rotherhithe to discharge.

Glengall Wharf, Millwall, with its tell-tale storage tanks and piles of barrels, traded as Thames Oil Wharf Co. Ltd

Prowess continued her established pattern of trade. On 31st March she sailed to Zaandam returning in dense fog with orders for Glengall Wharf, Millwall to discharge, both to the wharf and

into the barge *Eastward*. They had to await the flood tide to get away, with the barge in tow, for Younghusband's Wharf, Rotherhithe. The same round trip was repeated on 6th 14th, 21st and 30th April, then on 5th May, sailing again to Zaandam on 11th May arriving in dense fog at Ijmuiden at 10.20 a.m. to 'dress the ship over-all with flags owing to the day being the occasion of the King's Coronation', as the log records. There was little time to celebrate as the Pilot was soon aboard to proceed to the locks and to moor at Harts Fabriek at 2 p.m. to load.

Prowess was under way for Hull at 6.15 p.m. next day but more dense fog reduced her speed and delayed her arrival at Seatons Wharf to discharge. She then shifted to British Oil & Cake Mills berth to commence loading soya bean oil for Erith, London, where *Prowess* arrived at 9.10 a.m. on Monday 17th May to unload her cargo. After one more voyage the Ship's

Prowess in Zaandam, dressed overall to celebrate the Coronation of H.M. King George VI on 12th May 1937.

Log reports engine trouble but, after discharging her oil, she returned to Greenhithe to clean her tanks and take on water from S.S. *Alchymist*, then load lubricating oil at Purfleet for Hull. The spring was spent making passages between Rotherhithe, Zaandam, Knollendam and Hull until *Prowess* went onto the shipyard for painting below the waterline and minor mechanical repairs. The work completed, with satisfactory trials on Saturday 3rd July, she returned to the cross channel linseed oil trade.

On 30th August at 6.50 p.m., *Prowess* had just passed out of the Ijmuiden locks when the engine silencer cover suddenly disintegrated. The ship stopped, then turned back to moor to the bank to assess the damage. Next morning Charlie contacted the owner's office to await instructions from England. It was decided to pack cement around the damaged silencer and while they waited for it to set the crew were engaged on deck in scraping and oiling the aft derrick. They were underway again at 7 a.m. on 1st September and alongside Younghusband's Wharf, Rotherhithe, by 11.30 p.m. the following evening to start discharge of the cargo. With her tanks empty, she returned to Greenhithe where shore engineers dismantled the damaged silencer cover. Repairs completed, they sailed for Zaandam for two more loads.

Ijmuiden Sea Locks could take the largest ships. Although this mid-1930s photo is given scale by the British oil tanker *Otterhound*, built by Haverton Hill Shipyard, Stockton on Tees in 1927, the ship dwarfed by the lock chamber, the control tower for the very much larger lock can be seen to the left of *Otterhound*.

An Everard tank-barge at Greenhithe.

The poignant entry that recorded the loss of Charlie's wife Ada was entered after his return to *Prowess*. He was married for just over three years.

Back at Greenhithe on Friday 24th September 1937, Capt. Fielder received orders to proceed to the Humber and up the Yorkshire Ouse to Olympia Mills at Selby to load ground nut oil. Forty-eight hours later the cargo was loaded and *Prowess* was underway back to Greenhithe where she discharged part of the cargo into the tank-barge *Diamond*, before moving to Silvertown in dense fog to wait on buoys before discharging the remainder of the cargo at John Knight's soap works on 29th September.

Abruptly, there is a change to the usual routine entries in the log. It records 'Myself being paid off from my ship owing to serious domestic trouble on this day'

81

40TH WEEK | MOON RISES 2.16 a.m. | MOON SETS 4.41 p.m.

SEPT.-OCT., 1937

SUN RISES 6.58
SUN SETS 6.41

30 THURSDAY (273-92)

On this Day. suffered the loss of my Darling wife at the hour of 5.30 pm. Bereavement. Being after a long & painful illness. (Good old Sailor) which she had suffered with a fortitude that would be very hard to report upon.
Ada Edith Fielder
who died on this day 1937. ; Hour being 5.30 pm
"Gone from me my Dear" But never to be forgotten
("Rest in peace.")
(until the Day breaks.)

OCTOBER 1 FRIDAY (274-91)
Oxford Michaelmas Term begins   Pheasant Shooting begins : ends February 1st
Boots The Chemists Dividends payable

The log remains silent save for an entry on Tuesday 5th October, 1937: 'On this day my late wife was interred at East Sheen Hammersmith Cemetery - At rest.'

Public records show that Ada died aged just 32 at 73 Riverside Gardens, Hammersmith, and was buried on 5th October 1937. Entry No.10811 records her burial in section A, plot 9, No.75; the same plot in which her first husband, Thomas Frederick Owen, had been laid to rest some 3 years earlier. It seems that very soon after Ada died, her previous husband's sister gathered up her nephews and nieces, including young June Fielder, who she took to her own home. It appears that Charlie Fielder never saw his daughter again.

For Wednesday 13th October the ship's log records: 'On this day received orders from London office to rejoin my ship at Hull, travelling by train from Kings Cross to Hull.'

Capt. Charlie Fielder arrived at Hull at 5.30 p.m. in advance of the *Prowess*. On Thursday he was able to report her lying in Hull Roads awaiting a berth in the Old Harbour. At 11.10 a.m. she was under way to moor forty minutes later alongside the bacon factory to await sufficient water in the Hull River to reach her destination. The breeze was light northerly and the weather cold on Friday when she was underway with the steam tug *Fairy* in attendance, to lie alongside Seatons Wharf and discharged the cargo, working through the night. The return down river started at 2.15 a.m. on Saturday 16th October to anchor in Hull Roads to await the arrival of the second engineer who was still to join the ship. From there *Prowess* made her way to Yarmouth Roads and thence to Antwerp to load linseed oil.

The voyage was completed early on Wednesday 20th, with some delay due to the seemingly ever-present engine troubles. Kattendijk Locks were cleared outward at 7.00 p.m., but fog delayed their sailing for London.

They remained at anchor in the River Schelde overnight, but were underway at 8.00 a.m. next morning, with the fog clearing, bound to Gravesend for Greenhithe for orders. *Prowess* bunkered at Purfleet, then sailed on to Rotherhithe to transfer the cargo into the barge *Nightwatch*. She was emptied by Saturday 23rd October, when the ship returned to Greenhithe to receive orders at 7.40 p.m. for Antwerp again.

An hour into the passage the Chief Engineer sustained a severe cut on his head while *Prowess* was passing through the Lower Hope. Charlie decided to turn his ship back for Greenhithe so that the engineer could be put ashore to receive medical assistance. At 11 p.m. he reported to the shore foreman and arranged for the engineer to see the doctor. In view of recurring engine problems, Charlie felt the need to arrange for a replacement engineer, the ship remaining at Greenhithe awaiting his arrival until Sunday, before resuming the passage to Antwerp next day, Monday, 25th October 1937.

The trip became even more delayed and eventful when later on that Monday they were forced to turn back again, this time for shelter from a southerly gale after a couple of hours making little headway. They remained at anchor by the Yantlet Sands in heavy seas until the conditions moderated, setting off again at 6.40 a.m. on Tuesday to anchor to await the flood tide for Flushing Roads on their arrival. Their linseed oil was loaded on Thursday and discharged after arriving at Rotherhithe the next evening. *Prowess* had to lie outside *Acclivity* and the cargo was discharged into her.

Capt. Fielder returned with the ship to Zaandam to load another linseed oil cargo but on arriving at Ijmuiden the Chief Engineer reported the engine head joint needed adjustment. A repair was completed on the canal bank before they left on Tuesday 2nd November for the Humber estuary. In the river fog forced them to anchor until the Pilot was able to come aboard to take them into the Old Harbour. At

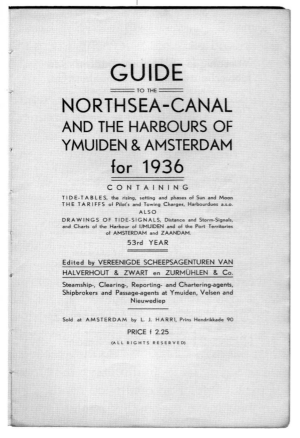

Charlie's copy of the Guide, published by the Dutch in English for the North Sea Canal. Despite the cost being the equivalent of just £1, it was not something he bought every year.

GUIDE
==== TO THE ====
NORTHSEA-CANAL
AND THE HARBOURS OF
YMUIDEN & AMSTERDAM
for 1936

CONTAINING
TIDE-TABLES, the rising, setting and phases of Sun and Moon
THE TARIFFS of Pilot's and Towing Charges, Harbourdues a.s.o.
ALSO
DRAWINGS OF TIDE-SIGNALS, Distance and Storm-Signals,
and Charts of the Harbour of IJMUIDEN and of the Port Territories
of AMSTERDAM and ZAANDAM.
53rd YEAR

Edited by VEREENIGDE SCHEEPSAGENTUREN VAN
HALVERHOUT & ZWART en ZURMÜHLEN & Co.

Steamship-, Clearing-, Reporting- and Chartering-agents,
Shipbrokers and Passage-agents at Ymuiden, Velsen and
Nieuwediep

Sold at AMSTERDAM by L. J. HARRI, Prins Hendrikkade 90

PRICE f 2.25

(ALL RIGHTS RESERVED)

Seatons Wharf, Thursday was spent discharging, then tank cleaning for a cargo of 230 tons of pella oil, a type used for grinding glass and stone. The persistent fog delayed departure, but when it had cleared sufficiently, Charlie was able to take *Prowess* south. They arrived at Glengall Wharf Millwall to discharge on Monday 8th November.

Trouble with the engine continued and, while at Greenhithe lying alongside *Alchymist*, the shore engineers dismantled the circulating pump while Lloyds Inspectors examined the life boats and passed the load line before they were able to fulfil orders to proceed to Zaandam. Strong northerly winds forced the ship to shelter, anchoring in the lee of the South Shoebury Sands. They took on water ballast there, but whilst so doing were requested to shift their anchorage by the military because of test firing from the Foulness ranges had *Prowess* in their line of fire! Although they got under way, they were again forced to seek shelter and signalled to Lloyds to report the delay to the owners. They reached their destination on Monday 15th, a week after her previous cargo was discharged, before loading linseed for Seatons, where they arrived on Wednesday, and where the ship was to remain until Saturday 20th November.

Charlie ordered the main engine be started for the return passage but, after several attempts, the Chief Engineer reported a complete loss of air and he was unable to start either the main or the auxiliary engines. Capt. Fielder went ashore to telephone the Everard offices to request any of the firm's fleet thereabouts to come to assist.

Later in the day *Apricity* arrived alongside and connected pipes to pump compressed air, used to start the engines, into *Prowess's* air bottles, before both ships got under way. On Monday *Prowess* ran into dense fog and anchored near the harbour. The Chief then reported he was unable to get the auxiliary engine working and later reported that the head had cracked beyond repair so they were now unable to discharge their ballast water. When they reached Zaandam they received instructions to engage a pumping barge to discharge the ballast before loading part of their cargo. Fog continued all day and night but it did not stop their move to another berth to top up the load to 210 tons.

Everard's dry cargo ship *Apricity*, built in 1933 at the same yard as *Prowess*, came to her assistance to start her engine. *Apricity* was long-lived, still in service for Greek owners in the early 1990s.

Next morning they were under way to Seatons where shore engineers from Greenhithe arrived to repair the auxiliary engine. The cargo was discharged, the tanks cleaned, but the move to Cleveland Mills on Tuesday 30th was thwarted by local barges getting stuck athwart the river as the tide left. When they reached the Mills the foreman rejected the *Prowess's* tanks which had to be steam cleaned before she could load 200 tons of 'washed cotton oil' for Jurgens Wharf at Purfleet. Back in the Thames on Friday 3rd December they started to pump out the oil, but the Chief Engineer reported that the auxiliary engine was overheating.

The unloading was suspended while shore engineers were again engaged to discover the cause. Pumping was resumed on Saturday morning using shore pumps, but these were unable to drain the tanks completely, so the ship was ordered to Greenhithe. A motor boat towed her down the Hull River before *Prowess* exited the Humber under her own power, arriving midday alongside at Greenhithe, the rest of the cargo discharged into the tank-barge *Windward*. The crew were scraping the tanks until 9 p.m. The ship's pump was still giving trouble and later stopped so it was again dismantled, the ships engineers working on it throughout the weekend. On Monday shore engineers re-assembled the auxiliary engine and refitted the air pump.

Prowess got under way with the crew washing out the cargo tanks. At 8.10 p.m. the main engine suddenly stopped and the Engineer reported that the fuel tank was empty! The reserve tank enabled the engine to be restarted and for them to make their way to Purfleet to refuel. *Prowess* returned to Greenhithe just before midnight.

At 7.00 a.m. on the morning of 7th December *Prowess* was under way through fog to Zaandam, for good measure encountering snow squalls and steep seas, the ship labouring heavily and making very little progress. Eventually they made their landfall at Ijmuiden, passing through the Sea Locks to Zaandam. While loading was under way the ship's Engineer overhauled the piston of the No.2 cylinder, but some hours after leaving Zaandam he reported a severe knock in No.3 cylinder so Prowess was moored to the canal bank whilst the problem was investigated. The Chief spent Saturday working on the engine, drawing and replacing the piston rings while the crew spent the time cleaning down the ship. Sunday, Monday and Tuesday, the ship lay weatherbound, although the crew were

The Canal Guide included a simple layout of the Zaandam Port Territory, which must have become a familiar sight for the crew of *Prowess*.

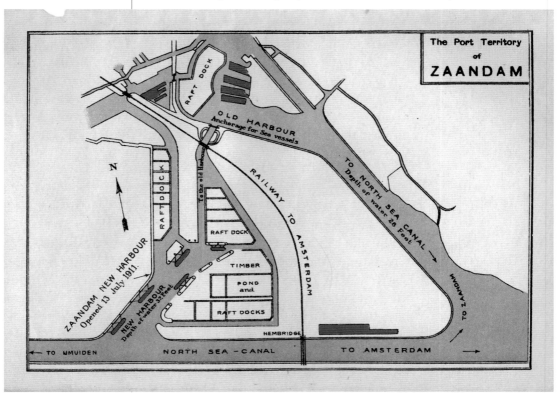

able to paint the hull, despite the wintry weather. On Wednesday 15th they were able to make their way through the locks and set off back to the Humber.

Just after midnight, in the early hours of Thursday, the main engine had to be stopped because the dynamo belt had broken. After half an hour they were under way for eleven hours to the Humber Light to be greeted by their Pilot with the news that a seafaring colleague of Charlie's had died after sustaining injuries while boarding a ship off Spurn Point. After discharging the cargo, the mate A.B. Cutler, gave notice to leave the ship (who could blame him) and on Saturday morning 20th December *Prowess* moored alongside to await the arrival of the repaired or replacement auxiliary engine cylinder head.

The 'spares' arrived, and they were under way at 4.40 p.m. for another, this time almost uneventful, passage to Holland returning to Younghusband, Barnes & Co.'s wharf at Rotherhithe to discharge, before moving to the Greenhithe Buoys, where *Prowess* was to lie alongside S.S. *Yantlet* for the Christmas holiday.

The whole weekend was cold with dense fog, hardly a cheering break for the very recently widowed Capt. Fielder, as he waited for a new mate to join him. On Monday 26th December, at midday, with the new mate aboard, they were under way for Zaandam, arriving at 2.40 p.m. on Tuesday to load linseed oil at Wormerveer and moor to the canal bank. The year, one of royal celebration for most, but deep sadness and sorrow for Charlie, ended with *Prowess* at anchor in the Thames Estuary in heavy rain squalls with seas breaking aboard, whilst awaiting a fair tide for London.

....

On Charlie Fielder's return to his Hammersmith flat he found a letter dated 28th December 1937 from his employer, Miss Annie Ethel Everard, a director of F.T. Everard & Sons Ltd., had written to advise that from 1st January 1938 the company had decided to contribute towards a pension scheme for its ship's officers which involved a contribution from each of them of nine pence in the pound. The company was at this time still very much a family firm, with the directors knowing their employees as individuals and it seems likely that Charlie was angry having not been consulted before the new pension arrangements were imposed in his absence, whilst afloat in command of *Prowess*.

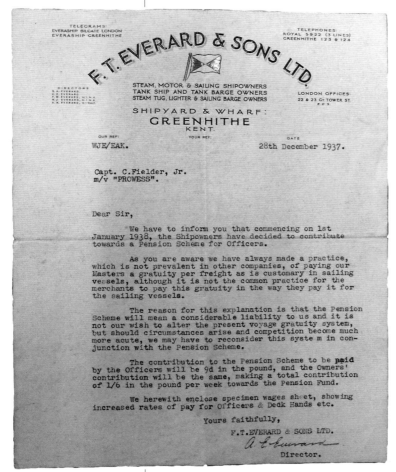

The letter found awaiting Charlie's return home from the *Prowess* after Christmas.

The Everard brothers were well known as employers who expected the best from their crews and, whilst treating them fairly according to their legal rights, were not considered by all as particularly generous. But shipping between the wars was a perilous business, only the commercially aware and hard-nosed ship owners surviving the slump in the British economy, many other companies going to the wall.

Despite the ship being just eleven years old, she had worked hard and it was clear that much of *Prowess's* machinery was worn out. The weather through the winter to date had been terrible. Both were factors which affected the earnings of the ship and the pressures on her Master, so there were grounds for dissatisfaction on both sides. Add to this the fact that Charlie had just lost his wife and, in effect, his daughter, there were clearly many reason's to wonder if the pension terms were the final straw, but Charlie parted company with F.T. Everard & Sons Ltd. and cleared his things from the ship, including the diaries and note books from which this account has been derived.

The Hammersmith Borough Council had pressed forward with their plans to improve their riverside and in 1936, despite legal problems and expense, had abandoned the proposal for the Brook Green site for their new town hall. They decided to erect a new Town Hall between Riverside Gardens and the Regal Cinema at the cost of £200,000. The foundations were excavated and a ceremonial stone was laid on the 2nd July, 1938 when the steelwork structure was already in place. The new Hammersmith Town Hall was completed in 1939.

During the building work the Fielder family continued to live in Riverside Gardens. Capt. Charlie Fielder returned to Flat 73 where, following the death of his wife Ada, he had been accepted as sole tenant. Charlie's brother George and his wife, Dinah (as Rosina, née Haysman, wished to be known), obtained the tenancy of Flat 110 around 1935. George applied to Watermans Hall on 12th November, 1937 to become a lighterman and his name was entered in the Book of Contract Bindings, on 14th December, 1937. He had no children and later moved to nearby Flora Gardens, but was unwell for some years and died of cancer in his fifties. Charlie's younger brother, Henry Thomas (Harry) and sister Emily Lydia also gave number 110 as their home address at this time.

The Port Line's S.S. *Port Hunter* sank, not as Charlie had recalled 'in the Indian Ocean', but in the North Atlantic, on 11th July 1942. There were just 3 survivors; they did not include Philip Henry Jones, Emily's husband, just 25, who was serving aboard as an Ordinary Seaman.

Charlie later mentioned Emily in his letters to Coast & Country Magazine. "My sister had been working on the big liners as a member of the laundry staff and was aboard *Orcades* on her maiden voyage. She married one of the stewards at Sydney and when the war came she left the sea to have her two sons, both of whom went to sea. Her husband was one of the 88 lives lost when the S.S. *Port Hunter* was torpedoed in the Indian Ocean."

Charlie's father also continued to give Flat 110 as his home address although Capt. Fielder Snr. was still working for Everard and would have often been away serving as Master of the sailing barge *Agnes Mary*. On 28th September 1938, when he was aged 64,

Her Majesty, built 1897, seen in Margate when she was the local 'Hoy', operating a time-tabled 'parcels' service from there to London, until purchased by Everard in 1918.

he was appointed Master of the sailing barge *Her Majesty* for a couple of weeks, before returning to his previous command to work out his time before retirement.

On 28th January 1938 Charlie Fielder was appointed temporary Master of Metcalf's tanker, *Frank M*. He took charge on Saturday 29th January at £6 a week with a cargo bonus of £1, he was told, for at least two weeks. He was to load at Thames Haven with motor spirit for Anglo American Oil Co. for delivery to their depot at Northam, Southampton and return to Thames Haven to load again for Northam. However, J.R. Wood, the fuel factors, advised a change of plan;

Metcalf's origins go back to 1893, but the operation of W.W.I X-Lighters secured their place in the coastal trades. Their first 'ship', in 1929, was the motor tanker *Frank M* which Charlie was briefly to command in 1938.

142

Frank M was to load for Jersey. Metcalf wrote on 4th February 1938, sending a cheque for £14.5s.6d. having sent £5 to the wives of Tomlinson and Allen (presumably his crew) confirming the instructions and insisting that he must make the Tuesday morning tide at St. Helier, as the brokers had telephoned to advise of the smaller tides after the 8th. Then, on 9th February, the owners wrote to advise that Capt. Mann, the *Frank M*'s regular Master, was fit for work and would be taking over on arrival at Purfleet. Capt Fielder was to call at the Metcalf office with the ships' papers and pratique. Afterwards, Charlie returned home to Hammersmith.

Capt. Charles Henry Fielder may well have contemplated the fact that, during his short time married to Ada, he had been

Charrington's lighter roads in the Thames.

away at sea for much of their marriage. Whatever his reason, he decided to give up seafaring at the age of 36 and return permanently to Hammersmith and to work on the river for Charrington, Gardner, Lockett (London) Ltd. He decided to follow his brother into lighterage and on 28th February 1938, applied to the Watermans Company of the River Thames for a special Lighterman's License. This was granted to him on 8th March 1938 and was Number 2701.

[1] Bagasse is the fibrous remains left after the extraction of the sugar-bearing juice from sugar-cane. It is a French word derived from the Spanish 'bagazo', meaning rubbish or waste.

Charrington were coal and coke merchants, formed in 1731 and headed up by five generations of men, all named John Charrington. The firm were one of the oldest lighterage companies operating on the Thames and associated waterways, with a fleet of barges, tugs, and hatch-craft carrying such diverse cargoes as oil, timber, bagasse[1] machinery and chemicals, with acknowledged speed and efficiency. They also had a number of estuarial oil tankers operating between Coryton Refinery and their fuel depot at Poplar. According to the original register of the Thames Conservators, who administered the tidal river between 1894 and 1909, Charrington's predecessors, Gardner, Lockett, Hinton Ltd. of

Mile End Commercial Wharf, were registered on 2nd March 1904 as owners of numerous canal barges, open barges and skiffs, having merged with an older firm, Gardner, Tomlin & Co. Ltd also of Mile End, Barge Owner No.110, who were registered with the Conservancy on 17th January1895.

The Second World War was soon to break out and affect the life of everyone on the river and in the country. Charlie appears to have been part of the Special Temporary Naval Service during W.W.II, but his service record remains a mystery. His family have a photograph of him in his naval uniform, including his cap with the H.M.S. band, no ship's name included for security and possibly economical reasons. When war was declared, Charlie's brother Wally, then aged twenty, had joined his father on the sailing barge *Agnes Mary* and gave his address as 'care of F.T. Everard'.

Capt. Charlie Fielder photographed in Royal Navy uniform.

It was wartime; Wally, with his father Charles Fielder Snr. in command, took cargoes of cement for the construction of the north shore buttress of the new Waterloo Bridge, the construction of which was disrupted by German bombing, the only Thames bridge to be hit during W.W.II. Wally recalls that "As we had to moor across the tide, the spring ebb used to make the *Agnes Mary* list right over. We also took a lot of cargoes to the Medway area where my mother had come from.

"During his school holidays, Tony Farnham used to come away with us on the barge, he was only about 12 at the time. He was a keen lad, always willing to learn the tricks of the trade. My dad and I always got on well with him. He knew all the old time skippers in the barge fleet in the village and they always spoke well of him. He went on to sail with Bob Roberts on *Greenhithe* and Cully Tovel on *Cambria*.

"During this time, my brother George, who was a very

talented man, taught me to play red sails in the sunset on a piano accordion. I was not very good. We had to move the *Agnes Mary* to the south side into a rubbish dump berth. As Dad and I had not been home for quite a while, we went home to Hammersmith. When we got back to the barge, we found that the cabin had been broken into and all our gear had been stolen, including the accordion, so I didn't have any more practice after that."

Wally remained as mate until around 1944, when 14 year old Jack Flint took his place but, as they were only working in the Thames and Medway rivers, the half yearly returns give no indication of the freights, cargoes or passages. Capt Fielder Snr.'s home address is given in the returns as 110 Riverside Gardens. Wally briefly became skipper of *Agnes Mary* before she was broken up at Greenhithe in March, 1953, but with sail in its last throes he moved into Metcalf's coasters, which his brother Charlie had briefly experienced some years earlier.

Meanwhile Charlie had received a letter, dated 15th June 1942, from J.D. Ritchie of the London Port Emergency Committee recording his recent enrollment in the service and confirming that the National Dock Labour Corporation gave an assurance that port transport workers would be entitled to resume their positions on the live registers on discharge (except for those guilty of misconduct) and return to their pre-service work. The letter also undertakes that if men were taken prisoner or interned they would continue to receive pay at 15/- per day, but not the 4/6d. lodging and provision allowance.

Amongst Charlie's belongings was a copy of Tide, Distance & Speed Tables for 1941, published by Henry Hughes & Son, probably issued to him and bearing the stark warning that it was not to be taken or sent abroad without appropriate authority.

Charlie remained on his own at 73, Riverside Gardens, until the summer of 1942 when, at the age of 39, he married Lily Elizabeth Haysman, the younger sister of George's wife Dinah. Lily had been born on 12th January, 1907 and was at the time living in Flat 203 and was working as a lamp assembler in an electrical works. They were married by special License in the King Street Registry Office on 11th July, 1942 with Lily's sister Ida as one of the witnesses. Lily's other sisters were Daisy and Violet Elizabeth, whose daughter Glynis believes that her aunt Ida died of tuberculosis during the war.

At the end of the W.W.II Charlie was still working for Charrington. In the immediate post-war barge registers of the P.L.A., the company was listed as Barge Owner No.8 and their fleet occupied some nine pages (folios.75/86). Many, if not the majority, of their barges were stem-head canal craft, with a single towing bollard on the foredeck (as seen in the photograph on p.143). The organisation also owned 91 river barges, including 59 wooden craft built between 1922 and 1927, a good proportion of which were sold to J.W. Hughan & Co. Ltd. on 16th December 1954, although many others were just broken up. The river lighters were both stem-headed and open (presumably swim-headed) and varied in size; 87'6" x 15' x 4'10" (probably used on the River Lee Navigation); 76' x 17'6" x 5'9" (probably used on the Grand Surrey Canal) and up to 90'3" x 23'11" x 8'4". The last craft, registered in 1955, was the

Pembury, No.17768, her dimensions 87'6" x 16'8" x 5'5", of 61.1 Registered Tons, 102 tons burden. The previous four; two pairs, *Tope* and *Tiff*, Nos.17548 and 17549, and *Tarn* and *Troy* Nos.17583 and 17584, each 87'6" x 22'2" x 7', of 122 Registered Tons, 204 ³/₄ burden.

Of their tugs, *Charlight* No.697, was[2] 44·10' x 12·5' x 4·2', registered on 9th March 1944, apparently a canal motor tug, while their steam tug *Charlock* No.455, was 71·0' x 18·1' x 8·6', registered on 14th September 1928, was from her dimensions clearly a river tug and was registered as a British Ship in the Mercantile Registry, Off. No.160589. They also had a new small canal tug, the *Regent*, No. 859, 33·0' x 8·8' x 3·8',

Charrington, Gardner, Lockett (London) Ltd. had the lighterage steam tug *Charlock*.

registered on 23rd June 1952 and the much larger river motor tug, *Margaret Lockett*, No.834, dimensions 70·7' x 18·1' x 7·3' registered 13th May 1952 which was sold to Everard in 1970 and renamed *P.B. Everard*.

[2.] Whereas the company's lighters were measured and recorded according to the original protocol of the Thames Conservators, in feet and inches, the tug's dimensions are recorded in feet and tenths of a foot, as is the custom with British Registered Ships.

Charlie joined in with staff excursions and on one occasion was photographed with his colleagues alongside their coach. He took an active interest in trade union activities, keeping virtually all the contribution cards issued by the Watermen, Lightermen, Tugmen & Bargemen's Union from 1920 to 1948. He also kept a print of the White Paper of 1946 from the Ministry of Labour and National Service, Port Transport Industry, report of inquiry; a foolscap draft of the Agreement between Master Lightermen's

A Charrington's staff outing, Charlie Fielder sporting a Trilby hat, smoking his pipe, sixth from the right of the photograph.

Union and the Transport & General Workers Union on the 'Rough Goods Lighterage Trade, Working Agreement and Rates of Pay, 1948'. His papers also included the extract from transcript of evidence by Brother W. Lindley of the Watermen, Lightermen, Tugmen & Bargemen's Union, to the Court of Inquiry, on 20th and 21st October 1954. Another document he kept was the Terms of Decasualisation Agreement of 6th September 1967. He also appears to have had a keen interest in trade union history, keeping 'Blood Red Roses, the supply of Merchant Seamen in the 19th Century' by Stephen Jones and from the same author, David & Charles' maritime history, entitled 'Community and Organisation, Early Seamen's Trade Unionism on the North East Coast, 1768 - 1844', hardly, one can imagine, light reading material.

Although no longer going to sea, Charlie Fielder retained a great interest in sailing barges, undaunted by his somewhat repetitive time in *Hilda*, or his experience of towing the sailormen in the Everard fleet while on *Prowess*. He acquired the first Journal of the Thames Barge Sailing Club in the summer of 1948 and also kept the promotional leaflet of the Sailing Barge Preservation Society, with the appeal by Sir Alan Herbert, in 1954. In all probability he attended the Thames Sailing Barge Match on Tuesday 19th June, 1956

and the 48th Medway Match the following Thursday, the programmes for which he retained. His former employers, F.T. Everard & Sons Ltd., were the main protagonists in these events, where their barges were pitted against those of their commercial rival, The London & Rochester Trading Company Ltd. of Strood on the River Medway.

His interest may have been heightened by his father's continuing service with F.T. Everard. The old Staff Record Cards were almost all destroyed as the company adopted more up to date means of data management. They had been stored in the basement of Woodlands below the former post office at Greenhithe which, by 1980 had been left boarded up. The card for Charlie's father 'Fielder, Charles Snr' had ended with the typed record

Sara represents the Everard company, and the traditions of British seafaring at the Festival of Britain, for which Charlie Fielder Snr. was appointed temporary Master.

'12.10.38 Agnes Mary, Capt.', but there was another hand written entry to record his appointment to the sailing barge *Sara* for the 1951 Festival of Britain where, dressed overall, she lay just ahead of a pair of narrowboats, a little way upstream of Hungerford Bridge, off the festival site.

Capt. Fielder was kitted out with a brass buttoned jacket and tie with a peaked cap emblazoned with gold braid and the company's house flag. *Sara* was the company's contribution to the exhibition and Charlie's father remained aboard during her time on the buoys, while crowds crossed over Hungerford Bridge to the Dome of Discovery, the Skylon, the nearby Sea and Ships pavilion and the delights of the South Bank Exhibition. There is just one further neat handwritten entry; in the 'date left' column is the date '26.11.53' and the remark 'died'.

Prowess on the yard after W.W.II.

As for *Prowess*, after the mechanical problems she had encountered during the time Charlie Fielder was her Master, it was perhaps only to be expected that during 1938, when just twelve years old, she was re-engined with a 4 cylinder, two stroke, single acting, 'F' type oil engine by Newbury Diesel Co. and put back in service.

In 1939, B. Seaman was appointed Master and later in that year A. Dyble joined as mate. At the end of the war in 1945 Dyble became her Master, a command he held for at least five years. In addition to the Deck Officers, A.B.s and O.S.s, her crew by then included 'Boys' who were paid £2.10s.2d compared with the Chief Engineers weekly wage of £10.8s.2d.

Her aging structure, not helped by a rusting 'Everard grey' painted hull, seen at Shoreham, just three years before the breaker's torch.

Although a British Registered Ship and considered a 'ship' by her owners and crew, in 1954 she was re-classified as a barge by the Port of London Authority and allotted their Official Number, 17687, which was to be displayed with her Owners' Number 1771. This somewhat demeaning designation was also suffered by other Everard motor tankers, *Affirmity*, P.L.A. No.17686, the *Aptity*,

No.17690 and the *Azurity*, No.17730, and the smaller 100 ft. former military steam tank barges *Apexity* and *Attunity*.

A Crew List for 1955 shows that *Prowess* maintained her old pattern of trade to the continent under Capt. Frank Stanislas of Brighton, but with a Master Mariner, G.M. Thomas as mate, she was now crewed by a succession of apprentices, under 18 years old, as evidence of her use as a school ship, with some financial benefit to the company as a result. *Prowess* remained in the Everard fleet until sold to A.E. Peirce of Canvey Island in 1961, before being sold on in March, 1962, to N.V. Machine & Scheepsloperij 'De Kooperhandel' for breaking up at Niew Lekkerland, Holland. The last entry in the Register for *Prowess*, Off. No. 149,707, reads 'Certificate cancelled and Registry closed this 3rd day of April, 1962 - Vessel broken up - Advice received from beneficial owner. This was not quite the end it appears, for a little of *Prowess* lived on. Before she was sold, her wheelhouse was cut off and taken ashore, probably to allow easy removal of her engine for refurbishment and further use, or for spares. It was put close to the slipway where it served as a paint store until the yard closed many years afterwards.

As for the Hammersmith Creekside, after a flying bomb devastated the last remnants of Little Wapping in 1944, Furnivall Gardens was created on the site in 1951. The Great West Road was built a few years later between the riverside and King Street, just a few feet from Riverside Gardens, cutting Rivercourt Road in half. The riverfront was no longer industrial but became instead a place where people might walk and enjoy the river views.

As for the family, with the departure from Flat 110 Riverside Gardens of brother Henry, sister Lydia and Gordon's marriage to 'Dolly' (Doris), the Electoral Roll records that George and Dinah (Rosina) remained at the flat. In 1953 Charlie's youngest brother Walter John (Wally) came to the flat for the remaining time their father lived there. Gordon and Dolly left the family flat and were shown in the electoral roll as living at No.12, in

Like *Prowess*, the *Apexity* was re-classified as a barge, as was the firm's *Azurity*, a tanker three times her size!

Block B, in 1969, with their son Peter and daughter Geraldine. Peter was absent from 1979 and his parents had left the flat by 1981. Although he had not 'gone on the water' he did look after the boats at the St. Paul's School boathouse on the Surrey Bank opposite the Upper Mall.

Charles and Lily had no children, but their flat, No.73, had two bedrooms so their niece Glynis was in the habit of going round to stay with them. Indeed, Glynis came to regard her uncle with much affection and when aged 10 or 11 she would go to see him when she heard he would be passing under Hammersmith Bridge. She could wave to him and his fellow lightermen on their tug and lighters as they passed beneath. Glynis recalls her uncle speaking of his carrying oil to Windsor Castle and seeing the Royal Family pass by in their car but there are no records of his work like that which has survived from his days in Everard coasters.

In later years, particularly when Lily was away, perhaps visiting her friends in Clacton, Glynis went to the Flat to see her uncle back after a late turn. Sometimes it would be well after midnight before he would return. With freezing hands and feet in his thick socks, he would sit by the fire to warm himself and have a late supper, perhaps an eel pie and mash from his favourite shop in Shepherds Bush. He might not get to bed until around two o'clock in the morning, but had still to be up by five next day to start work again.

Sometime around 1971 Charles retired from the water at the age of 68 and had his retirement gathering at the London Apprentice pub by the Thames in Isleworth, past which he had often travelled, with many of his colleagues from Charrington present for the party. He somewhat regretted having to accept retirement, but spent much of his time reading about the river and engaging in correspondence with old colleagues and the press including a succession of letters to Paddy O'Driscoll, the Editor of East Coast Digest, or Coast & Country as it became.

At Christmas, or for his birthday, Glynis and her family would present him with a bottle of vintage port 'to clear the bronchial tubes' as he would say. He still kept in touch with his colleagues from his days with Everard and in August, 1976, he wrote to East Coast Digest: 'Dick, the Dagger, Capt. Miller, was a personal friend of myself and family. I paid him a visit on the occasion of his 100th birthday (I myself am only 73). We reminisced of old times, Dick was at one time skipper of a Scandinavian built barge and I was amazed by his vigour and ease of getting about. He had a great sense of humour and I much regret hearing of his death.'

Charlie and Lily stayed in their flat, No. 73, in Block I, until 1980, when they moved into the single bedroom Flat 90, where Glynis, who had married and had her own family nearby, continued to visit them, often twice a day. Late one evening in October 1993, Lily rang her niece to plead for her to come round quickly to help her uncle who had been taken ill. Glynis called an ambulance to take him to Charing Cross Hospital in Fulham, where he died on 8th October, having suffered an acute heart attack.

Charles was always a perfect gentleman, he was a prolific letter writer and could talk on many subjects including sport, particularly football and his support for Fulham Football Club. Sometime later Lily asked Glynis to take down a battered brown suitcase from the top of a wardrobe in their bedroom and gave it to Glynis. It contained Charlie's archive. Glynis also gathered together the various books he had collected, especially those dealing with Kent, barges and the sea, many of which she and her husband had given as presents. She wanted to find a good home for the many things in the suitcase and went onto her computer where she found the Twickenham Museum had a website concerned with the river.

The suitcase had fallen to pieces, but its contents were gathered into a plastic bag. Glynis went to the Museum, near St. Mary's Church and the slipway into the river, coincidentally near to a working lighter alongside the Embankment, hard by where Charlie and the many thousands of lightermen that preceded him, must have worked on their way upriver. She handed the bag to a volunteer at the museum, but the management there had to conclude that, while the archive was of some significance, it was not within their collection policy and should be held elsewhere.

Elsewhere turned out for much of it to be the National Maritime Museum, Glynis signing the accession document, the arrangements having been made by David Wood of The Society for Sailing Barge Research, for whom the preparation of this publication has been a five year journey. ◊

153

This Transcript of Register indicates the Everard shareholding in the *Prowess* at 74 sixty-fourths! This must be a mistake by the transcriber, as there cannot be more than 64 shares in a British Registered Ship, though each share can be owned by more than one shareholder.

Prowess was George Brown & Co.'s Yard No. 154, with a 200bhp 4 cylinder two stroke Single Acting 'P50 type' oil engine by Plenty & Co. Ltd., Newbury, built under License to a 1910 design by Kromhout of Rotterdam.

LLOYDS REGISTER supplement +100A1 at Lloyds, machinery aft, QD 33' - F 14' - 104'3" x 23'0" x 9'0" 7 BH (bulkheads), FPT (fore peak tank) 8t, APT (aft peak tank) 18t, - Coils (heating coils), summer freeboard 7½".

PLA Owners No. 1771, Barge Register No. 17687, Tonnage 77m 128 b. Length 106¹/₁₀' x 23²/₁₀' x 9'.

Form No. 19.   Signal Letters (if any) M.P.F.R.

Transcript of Register for Transmission to Registrar-General of Shipping and Seamen.

Official Number	Name of Ship	No., Date, and Port of Registry
149707	Prowess	114 in 1926 London

No., Date and Port of previous Registry (if any)

Whether British or Foreign Built	Whether a Sailing, Steam or Motor Ship; if Steam or Motor Ship, how propelled	Where Built	When Built	Name and Address of Builders
British	Motor Ship Single Screw	Greenock	1926	Geo Brown & Co Greenock

		Feet	Tenths
Number of Decks — One	Length from fore part of stem, under the bowsprit, to the aft side of the head of the stern post	106	1
Number of Masts — One	Length at quarter of depth from top of weather deck at side amidships to bottom of keel		
Rigged — Smack	Main breadth to outside of plank	23	2
Stern — Elliptical	Depth in hold from tonnage deck to ceiling at midships	9	1
Build — Clincher	Depth in hold from upper deck to ceiling at midships, in the case of three decks and upwards	—	—
Galleries — None	Depth from top of beam amidships to top of keel	9	5
Head — None	Depth from top of deck at side amidships to bottom of keel	9	1.6
Framework and description of vessel Steel Oil Tanker	Round of beam	—	—
Number of Bulkheads Seven	Length of engine room, if any	24	—
Number of water ballast tanks, and their capacity in tons Two - 26 Ton			

PARTICULARS OF DISPLACEMENT.

Total to quarter the depth from weather deck at side amidships to bottom of keel ... 343 Tons. Ditto per inch immersion at same depth ... 4.75 Tons.

PARTICULARS OF PROPELLING ENGINES, &c. (if any).

No. of sets of Engines	Description of Engines	Whether British or Foreign made	When made	Name and address of makers	Reciprocating Engines		Rotary Engines	N.H.P.
					No. and Diameter of Cylinders in each set	Length of Stroke	No. of Cylinders in each set	B.H.P. I.H.P. Speed of Ship
One	Internal Combustion Semi-diesel	British	1926	Plenty & Son Ltd Newbury	Four		—	—
No. of Shafts One	Particulars of Boilers Description Number Iron or Steel Loaded Pressure				335 ⁷/m	590 ⁷/m	—	200
								7½ Knots

PARTICULARS OF TONNAGE.

GROSS TONNAGE.	No. of Tons	DEDUCTIONS ALLOWED.	No. of Tons
Under Tonnage Deck	167.63	On account of space required for propelling power	92.52
Space or spaces between Decks		On account of spaces occupied by Seamen or Apprentices, and appropriated to their use, and kept free from Goods or Stores of every kind, not being the personal property of the Crew. These spaces are the following, viz.:—	19.50
Turret or Trunk			
Forecastle	6.99		
Bridge space		In Forecastle and Deck House	
Poop or Break	19.53		
Side Houses	.64	(Number of seamen or apprentices for whom accommodation is certified ...)	
Deck Houses	9.62		
Chart House		Deductions under Section 79 of the Merchant Shipping Act, 1894, and Section 54 of the Merchant Shipping Act, 1906, as follows:—	
Spaces for Machinery, and light and air, under Section 78(2) of the Merchant Shipping Act, 1894			
Excess of Hatchways	2.50	Cubic Metres. Master Accommodation 2.58	17.80
Gross Tonnage	206.91	585.56 Water Ballast Space	
Deductions, as per contra	129.82	867.40	Total 15.42
Register Tonnage	77.09	218.16	129.82

NOTE.—1. The tonnage of the engine room spaces below the upper deck is 52.87 tons, and the tonnage of the total spaces framed in above the upper deck for propelling machinery and for light and air is 9.69 tons.

NOTE.—2. The undermentioned spaces above the upper deck are not included in the cubical contents forming the ship's register tonnage:

Name of Master		Certificate of Service No. / Competency No.

Names, Residence, and Description of the Owners, and Number of Sixty-fourth Shares held by each} viz.,

F. T. Everard & Sons Limited having its principal place of business at The Wharf, Greenhithe in the County of Kent.

Shares - Seventy four.

William Joseph Everard of Accaba House, High Street Greenhithe, Kent

Dated for Certificate annexed   Registrar.

NOTE.—Registrars in the Colonies are requested to distinguish the Managing Owner by placing the letters "M.O." against his name.

C. No. 345.

N.B.—To be sent in an envelope addressed to the Registrar-General of Shipping and Seamen, Tower Hill, London, E.C.3.

Instructions to Registrars of British Ships, para. 32.—Sec. 85198/1933

(1668). *M.10405/1234. 5/36. 5,000. A.H.665.

Re-engined 1938 with 4 cylinder 2 stroke Single Acting 'F type' oil engine 240 x 345 by Newbury Diesel Co. Sold to A.E.Peirce of Canvey Island 1961, resold to N.V.Machine & Scheepsloperij 'De Kooperhandel' for breaking up at Niew Lekkerland, Netherlands, in March, 1962.

The typewritten Specification provided to F.T. Everard & Sons Ltd. for the construction of the Motor Tanker *Prowess*, by George Brown & Co. Ltd., Greenock, in 1926, (Yard No.154)

Footnotes referenced within the document appear at the end of the Specification.

Thanks to the Mitchell Library, Glasgow City Archives for provision of this data.

================

HULL SPECIFICATION

OF A

STEEL SCREW MOTOR VESSEL

FOR THE

CARRIAGE OF OIL IN BULK.

===============

<u>DIMENSIONS</u> :-

        Length between perpendiculars.............. 105'0"

        Breadth moulded....................................... 23'0"

        Depth moulded... 9'0"

<u>GENERAL DESCRIPTION</u> :-

        The vessel is to be built with engines aft and rigged with one mast. To carry about 210 tons oil, (but not less than 200 tons) at 41 cubic feet per ton and 25 tons of bunkers, stores or other deadweight on Lloyd's Freeboard about 8'2". Speed about 7 knots on trial loaded with 200 B.H.P. (Deadweight for trial to be supplied by Owner). To have raised Quarter Deck, Bridge with Mess-room, and Officers' accommodation. Crew in Monkey Forecastle as per plan.

        The oil space to be divided as per plan into Six Oil tanks[1] and cofferdam. All bulkheads of tanks and cofferdams to be oil tight work, and cofferdam bulkheads to be continuous from side to side and full depth of tanks.

        The oil tanks to be arranged below the main deck, with separate trunk hatches for expansion.

        Vessel to be built of steel under special survey and classed 100 A.1. at Lloyd's. Such parts as Rules permit may, if practicable, be of iron. All requirements of the registry to be carried out.

<u>ACCOMMODATION</u> :-

        The Mess Room to be lined with pine, with pitch pine dining table and sideboard, cushioned settee, mirror, and timepiece. Captain's room to have fittings of mahogany bed with drawers under, wardrobe, sofa seat, wash-stand with plug basin, jug and receiver, folding table top, chair, toilet rack, mirror and clothes pegs. The underside of the deck to be painted. Bulkheads and side lining of pine, painted or grained and varnished.

        Officers' rooms to have pitch pine fittings, bed and drawers, cushioned settee, wash basin, with table top, mirror and clothes pegs. Painted or grained as above. Bogie stoves to be fitted in Cabins and Mess-room and larger one with ring for cooking in Forecastle.

<u>ANCHORS AND CHAINS</u> :-

        As required by Lloyd's Rules.

        Cable ends to be secured by shackles with easy pins.

        One spare anchor shackle and two spare cable shackles to be provided.

<u>BELLS</u> :-

        One 9" Brass Ship's Bell in suitable iron stand with ship's name engraved.

<u>BOATS</u> :-

        To have one lifeboat and one open square sterned boat clinker built of Larch and copper fastened, fitted with yellow metal air chambers, placed on beams, as per plan. To have a complete set of ash oars, rowlocks, rudder, tiller, &c. and to comply in every respect with the Board of Trade Regulations.

<u>BLOCKS</u> :-

    All blocks to have patent Sheaves, and have internal binding.

<u>LONGITUDINAL BULKHEAD</u> :-

    All oil tight longitudinal bulkhead shall be fitted in each oil tank extending to the deck, extending through cofferdams, with efficient connections attends of vessel. 4" Sluice Valves to be fitted in this bulkhead and also in thwartship divisions of Tanks (4 valves in all).

<u>CARPENTER AND BOATSWAIN'S STORES</u> :-

    1 Flagstaff
    6 Handspikes
    Keys for all valves
    2 Chain Hooks
    2 Sounding Rods and Lines
    2 Shifting Spanners
    1 Log Line and Reel
    1 Japanned Lantern
    1 Vice and bench
    6 Marline Spikes
    6 Eyebolts
    1 Hand Lead, 10lbs and line
    1 deep sea lead, 42 lbs and line
    1 reel for deep sea line
    1 pair lamp tweezers
    1 deck socket with set of distress signals as required by Board of Trade
    12 Shackles (assorted)
    1 Shackle Hammer
    2 Cork Fenders with Lanyards
    2 Lifebuoys with ship's name or as required by Board of Trade
    Lifebelts as required by Board of Trade
    2 Shovels
    2 Deck Scrapers
    2 Deck Scrubbers
    2 Mops and handles
    3 Long Tar Brushes
    6 Paint brushes, assorted
    3 steel brushes
    6 paint pots
    1 pair lamp scissors
    1 tin oil feeder for lamps
    1 spring oil feeder for winch
    1 rigging screw
    1 pair luff tackle blocks with patent sheaves and falls
    3 spare blocks assorted (patent sheaves)
    2 iron snatch blocks with 5 inch sheaves
    2 heaving lines, 30 fathoms long

CAUTION PLATES :-

Two plates prohibiting the use of naked lights to be fitted up in prominent positions on deck.

CEMENTING AND TILING :-

Bottom of ship outside of the oil compartments to be cemented with Portland Cement and Sand. The floors of galley and W.C.'s to be cemented and tiled.

CERTIFICATES :-

Of classification, tonnage, chain and anchor testing to be handed to the Owners on delivery of vessel. Peak tank to be deducted from tonnage. Builder to pay all survey, Classification Registration Fees and Royalties. Vessel to be measured by Board of Trade at Builders' expense.

Builder to fully insure vessel to time of delivery against fire, trial trip and all other risks.

CHAIN LOCKER :-

To be fitted where shown of sufficient capacity to stow the bower cables. Chain pipes from windlass to be of steel.

COMPASSES :-

To have two compasses, viz, one Standard Compass in binnacle on Bridge, with lamps, and 9" Card. One 8" Card overhead compass in Captain's Room. All to be fitted and adjusted at expense of Shipbuilders. The above compasses to be by Dobbie & McInnes, or other equal Maker.

COOPERAGE &c :-

4 teak deck buckets with brass hoops and ship's name, stropped, with rack
6 Galvanized Deck Buckets

CREWS QUARTERS :-

To be arranged with metal beds, pine lockers, seats, table, mirror and coat pegs. All accommodation to be in accordance with Board of Trade requirements. No cleading [sic. cladding] to be fitted at ship's side. All iron work over bunks to be cork dusted and painted. Slow combustion stove with ash pan and funnel complete.

DECK FITTINGS :-

All skylights to be of steel or teak, with strong round plate glass lights in brass frames. Hatch bars to each exposed hatch fitted with wood covers, also set of battens and wedges. Store-room hatches, if any, to have locking bars and locks.

DECK GEAR :-

All portable gear to have proper places and fittings for securing them when not in use.

DECKS :-

Main deck to be of steel, not less than $^3/_8$" thick, and decks over bridge and forecastle to be of pitch pine in way of accommodation. Bolts of Galvanised iron, the heads well bedded and carefully dowelled, and to be properly caulked and payed with marine glue. All oil tight decks to be double riveted. Gunwhale bars on oil deck strongly riveted. Gunwhale bars on oil deck strongly riveted. A margin angle to be fitted round forecastle head forming waterway.

Forecastle deck to be of ⁵/₈" steel sheathed as above.

DECK BEAMS :-

In way of all decks angle beams to Lloyd's requirements to be fitted. Air relief holes through beams and carlings.

ELECTRIC LIGHT INSTALLATION :-

Electric Lights by Telford Grier & Mackay, to be fitted throughout the accommodation, crew's quarters, engine room and pump room, and other places where it is necessary to provide light, including Compass and telegraph, also two portable hand lamps for use in way of the oil compartments, with 60 feet of flexible cable each. Pilot light to be fitted on switchboard. Electric lighting plan is to be approved by owners, 2 cargo group lamps with 60 feet of flexible cable each, two connections for hand lamps and cargo lamps, fitted with watertight covers.

Switchboard to have necessary switches, fuses and volt and ampere meters, Port and Starboard lanterns to be fitted for electric light. Stern light aft. All cables to be armoured and well secured in place and the whole fitted on the return wire system. Masthead light to be fitted.

Lamp as required by Board of Trade when carrying petrol.

The main cables to be armoured, led along the ship in an approved manner.

Dynamo to be fitted at starting platform, fore and aft and to have governor, to be of ample power to drive all the ship's lights. All wired of ample size, lead covered or armoured, as required in accommodation. Portable lamp in engine room.

Lamps to have metal filaments.

Each lamp in accommodation and where required to have separate switch.

CASINGS :-

As per plan. A rail to be fitted on the engine room skylight to hold skylight flaps.

To have two doors to engine room.

ENGINE SEATINGS :-

To be arranged to suit Engineer's requirements. Thrust and Engine Seating to be well designed and constructed.

EXPANSION TRUNKS :-

To be arranged, as per plan, over the oil tanks, proper provision shall be made to allow for at least three per cent expansion. Portable covers to be hinged and fitted with usual plugs and escape cocks. Top covers to be fitted with brass nuts. Two hinged oil-tight manholes in each trunk with brass fly-nuts, ladder to be fitted and two 3" dip holes in each trunk.

FLAGS :-

1 National Ensign, 2 yards
1 Pilot Jack, 1¹/₂ yards
1 House flag, 1¹/₂ yards

1 Burgee 12" letters
To be supplied with suitable flag locker.

FRAMES :-
Side frames to be as required by Classification, with large limbers and freeing holes through floors.

FRESH WATER TANK :-
Two 150 gallon tanks placed in suitable positions on top of casing, fitted with filling and air pipes, draw-off pipes and cocks.

GALLEY :-
To have half iron doors and necessary dresser with drawers and lockers under, seat to be arranged, iron coal bunker, iron shelf and firing tools. One cooking range large enough to cook for all on board. Utensils, as per inventory.

GALLEY STORES :-
1 - 6 gallon C.I. oval pot
2 large iron kettles
1 tin fish kettle
2 iron saucepans and covers
2 frying pans (tinned)
1 meat saw
1 mincing block
1 mincing knife
1 copper kettle (2 quarts)
2 iron stew pans (tinned)
1 sea pie pan
1 cocks axe
1 Flour dredger
2 dripping pans
1 tin pail
1 grater
1 tormentor
1 gridiron
2 tin basins
1 cook's fork
1 soup ladle
1 pepper box
1 paste board
1 rolling pin
1 cook's knife
6 tin mess kids
2 tin teapots, enamelled
2 tin coffee pots, enamelled
1 steel
1 toasting fork
1 cook's spoon
1 gravy strainer

HATCHES :-

Bolted covers to be fitted to expansion trunks, with two hinged oil-tight manholes on top of each properly finished, with necessary fittings. Hatchways shown elsewhere to be not less than 30" high with wood covers. Double canvas covers both sets tarred to be fitted.

HAND PUMP :-

A portable pump to be supplied with two lengths interchangeable sections of 10 feet each, complete with strum, one length delivery, 25 feet.

IRON CASTINGS :-

Bollards and fairleads to be fitted where shown. Hawse pipes with deck plates and large rounded flanges outside, to be well fastened.

KEEL :-

Of flat steel plate not less than $^1/_2$" thick as required by Classification.

KEELSONS :-

Lower strake of centre bulkhead to be intercostal between Transverse bulkheads, and upper landing to come above top of floor knee angles.

Side Keelsons as required by Classification.

All bulkhead Keelson knees to be large and strongly riveted to bulkheads.

LADDERS :-

To be of iron to erections on deck. Galvanised iron handrails to be fitted to deck ladders. Two permanent iron ladders to be fitted to each oil compartment and cofferdam.

LAMP ROOM :-

Placed where shown fitted with drawer and the necessary shelves for ship's side lights, mast lights, &c. One 10 gallon oil tank of galvanised iron, with cock, key and filling plug.

LAMPS FOR CABINS, &c. :-

One brass hanging lamp for mess room, one brass bracket oil lamp for each Officer's and Captain's cabins, one japanned bulkhead reflector lamp for crew space, one for galley, one storm lantern, one davy lamp, and two brass bulkhead lamps for Engine Room.

LASHINGS :-

Spare Anchors to have band lashings placed as agreed on. Stream Anchor to be stowed aft.

All locks and hinges on wood work throughout the steamer to be of brass. All outside locks to be good lever pattern. Hooks and catches to be fitted to all doors. Iron doors to have hinges with brass pins and brass fitted galvanized locks.

MASTS AND SPARS :-

Mast to be of pitch pine and be made to lower. To be supported at Main deck in suitable socket. Lightning conductor to be fitted. Derricks with all necessary smithwork for rigging to be fitted, suitable for lifting a load of 30 cwts.

162

MOULDING :-

A 3" x 1¼" solid moulding to be carried alongside and round stern as per plan.

NAME :-

To be in large letters on each bow, and the name and port of registry on stern cut in.

OIL PIPING :-

The oil pipes to be of Cast Iron, having necessary expansion joints. The whole of the joints to be faced and bolted up in an efficient manner. Bends of cast iron. All fastenings through decks to have holes tapped.

To have a single 4" pipe line with master valves and discharge pipe as shown. Suitable connections to be made for jointing shore piping. Arranged for filling oil tanks as well as pumping out. Main lines to be 4" diameter with 4" branches to tanks. All pipes to be properly secured and stayed, iron only being used. Valves to be controlled from deck and to be interchangeable and of sluice type and to be actuated by screw on valve. All valves to be legibly marked and screw one way. sections to draw from after end, and close to centre line bulkhead in all tanks.

Valves and fittings to be cast iron with brass seats and valve spindles of Muntz Metal.

An extra 2" drain suction to be fitted to each tank.

A special plan of oil piping to be approved.

PAINTING AND CLEANING :-

All steel work to have two coats of oxide paint, and external parts two extra coats of approved colour. The deck work and accommodation to be finished in approved colours. The oil compartments to be scaled clean and brushed only.

All peaks and cofferdams to be cement washed.

PLATING :-

Shell plating to be lapped (not joggled) with all butts and landings arranged to Classification Requirements. All deck and shell seams in way of tanks to be double riveted.

PUMP ROOM :-

As per plan. To be built of steel with access door, round lights, &c.

PUMPS :-

One Steam driven[2] Tangye or other approved brass fitted oil pump to be supplied. Also a similar pump to be fitted below deck forward, see plan.

RAILS AND STANCHIONS :-

To be fitted where necessary.

Rails and stanchions within 6 feet of the Compass on bridge to be of brass.

RIGGING :-

All standing rigging to be of wire rope served 3 feet above the eyes and all stays, shrouds and backstays to be set up with screws to be made to lower with purchase blocks and falls.

All running gear to be of best manilla rope.

RIVETING :-

To Lloyd's requirements. Lap butts to be adopted as much as possible. Steel rivets in shell and deck.

ROPES :-

As required by Lloyd's.

All wire ropes to be supplied with a large mooring shackle each. Wires to have reels.

RUDDER :-

Forged rudder stock to be $\frac{1}{4}$" larger than Lloyd's requirements, with portable arms, plate to be riveted to arms, fitted with portable pintles. Wrought iron quadrant to be fitted on rudder head to take steering chains. Rudder to be arranged to draw Tail Shaft out aft.

SCUPPERS :-

To be ample, also all necessary scuppers from the deck erections and arrangements made for draining peaks, peak tops, chain locker, pump room, &c.

SIDE LIGHTS :-

For light and ventilation in the crew's quarters and each compartment of cabin accommodation. The lights to be 8" diameter in crew's quarters and 9" in the Cabins. These forward to be furnished with dead light covers on separate hinges and with portable plugs.

SIGNAL LAMPS :-

Set of side and masthead lamps of copper with dioptric lenses and silvered reflectors, stern and anchor lamps, also red globe lamp, all fitted for electric light. Cisterns fitted to Anchor and Red Globe Lamp for burning either paraffin oil or colza. Set of distress red globe lamps and black balls. All to be as per Board of Trade Regulations. Spare galvanised masthead, port, starboard and stern lights, for oil.

A cage to be supplied for oil masthead lamp.

STEERING GEAR :-

To have a hand gear of Messrs G & J McOnie, Fishers Ltd., or other equal make, and of sufficient size placed on bridge with necessary chains and $\frac{3}{4}$" rods leading to quadrant. Guards to be fitted on quadrant to prevent the chain jumping off. Tightening screws to be fitted as usual. Relieving tackle or spare hand tiller to be fitted aft. Plan of gear to be approved.

STEEL AND IRON WORK :-

To be of best quality and of such scantlings as will pass survey and attain stipulated Classification, the spacing of rivets and caulking to be of best description and carefully executed. All thwartship bulkheads and strengthening in oil tanks to be of steel. Sheer strake to be not less than $\frac{1}{2}$" thick.

STEM :-

Of best forged scrap iron or rolled steel not less than 6" x $1\frac{1}{4}$" well connected to keel and shell.

164

STERN FRAME :-

Of best forged scrap iron, with solid gudgeons formed on it to take rudder pintles, and fitted with hard steel washer on bottom pintle. Heel to be well rounded up. To have suitable aperture for Propeller, and boss for end of stern tube. Arranged for drawing Tail Shaft out aft.

STEWARD'S STORES :-

1 cloth brush
1 short brush
1 scrubbing brush
1 tea canister (7 lbs)
1 coffee canister (7 lbs)
1 tin opener
1 corkscrew
1 wash leather
1 sugar canister
1 knife board
1 wooden bread plate
1 dust pan
1 japanned water can
1 brass spittoon

STRINGERS :-

Side stringers as required by Classification to be fitted, and connected to thwartship bulkheads by strongly riveted heavy gusset knees and angles.

Stringers to be intercostal to bulkheads and web frames. Freeing holes out where required.

Bulkhead stringers to be strongly riveted to bulkheads.

UPHOLSTERY :-

Floor of Mess Room and Captain and Officers' rooms to be covered with linoleum. All windows to have curtains of repp or damask. Seats to have cushions stuffed with hair and covered with fancy repp or pegamoid; Two door mats to be supplied.

VENTILATORS :-

Placed in suitable positions as required by Owners. Four ventilators 8" diameter to Engine room, 9" ventilator to firemen's and seamen's compartment, 6" vents to pump room. The entire ventilation to be to Board of Trade requirements.

Pump Room Ventilators to have spark-proof screens over mouths.

All cofferdams to have gooseneck ventilators of 3" pipe, covered with spark-proof screens.

WATER CLOSETS :-

To have two valve closets for Officers and crew. The W.C.s to be flushed from the wash deck service pipe, which is to have a permanent connection with cock to overhead cistern. Sea valve to be fitted to all W.C.s.

WATER TESTING :-

The Oil Compartments and cofferdams to be tested before launching with a head of water as required by Lloyd's and under this condition to be absolutely watertight to the approval of Purchaser's inspectors. Each half-tank to be tested separately.

WINDLASS :-

To be a Steam Windlass[2] placed forward of Good & Menzies make with stoppers complete. Bed for windlass to be 2" think with a steel plate below deck, efficiently supported by pillars. Bow to be strengthened by breast hook, and thicker plating at hawse pipes.

GLASS & EARTHENWARE :-

6 breakfast cups and saucers
6 tea cups and saucers
4 basins
1 butter dish
6 soup plates
6 dinner plates
6 pudding plates
6 cheese plates
6 tea plates
2 oval meat dishes
2 vegetable dishes and covers
2 salts
6 egg cups
1 water jug
1 sugar basin
1 cream jug
6 tumblers

GENERALLY :-

The vessel to be fitted in every respect complete to this Specification, and as usual in vessels of this class and type, including all requirements of Lloyd's, the Board of Trade or Home Office, and Factory Acts, and no reasonable requirements of the Purchasers shall be withheld by the Contractors, provided such requirements do not involve additional cost.

The whole of the work to be to the reasonable satisfaction of the Owners and their surveyors.

One set of tracings of the general plan, ballast and pumping arrangement of ship as built to be supplied to Owners. Any detail plans required by the Owners of their Inspectors during construction to be supplied.

Plans of pumping arrangements, etc. also pipe plans and displacement calibration and capacity scales, to be framed and hung in the Mess Room.

The following tracings shall also be supplied:-

Displacement Scale showing Displacement, Dead weight Freeboard and Draft.

ADDENDA.

Heating Coils to be carried from centre line across bottom and up the sides of vessel to the underside of deck in each frame space, of 1¹/₂" solid drawn piping to be fitted in each Tank, so arranged that Steam may be taken from Shore connection, the inlets to be arranged on deck at junction of Tanks, the discharge for each Tank to be led out through side of expansion trunk with cock fitted. Packing of flanges and joints to be "Kimbala" as supplied by Beldams Asbestos Co., 71 Queen Street, Glasgow. Special Bulkhead flanges to be fitted where passing through decks or bulkheads, otherwise the system to be as in the [sic.]

FUNNEL :-

A hinged funnel to be fitted with silence box formed in Skylight over Engine Room, as per plan to be submitted.

House Flag on each side of funnel.

Gratings - Ladder and Flooring in Engine Room not supplied by Engineers to be fitted by Shipbuilders.

Hand Winch - A double purchase hand winch with warping ends and centre barrel to be fitted forward of Mast.

Capstan Aft - A strong Steam geared capstan to be fitted over Quadrant Aft.

Wash Port - Openings to be fitted with bars instead of Doors.

---

[1] The ship as built was to include 4 No. cargo tanks, not 6 No. as in this Specification. The undated General Arrangement drawing on pages 40/41 shows 4 No. cargo tanks.

[2] The inclusion of steam powered items of equipment within this Specification may be explained by the possibility that *Prowess* was originally envisaged as steam powered, not a motor tanker. This is quite possible given the success of the steam tankers already in the fleet and the benefits of being self-sustaining for discharge of cargo that needed heating to achieve sufficient liquidity for pumping ashore. Alternatively their inclusion could be as a result of standards for the shipyard in respect of these items, erroneously included. Obviously, though a shore based steam supply would be suitable for cargo discharge, it would not be suitable for the anchor windlass.

Passages undertaken
by Charles H. Fielder
aboard the
Motor Tanker
Prowess

1932
October
15	London - King's Lynn
	King's Lynn - molasses - Bergen o(p) Z(oom),
	The Netherlands
	(10 passages until year end)
	Bergen o Z - Cantley

1933
January
1	Cantley - Gt. Yarmouth, 2.1.33
2	Gt. Yarmouth - Cantley, 2.1.33
3	Cantley - molasses - Bergen o Z, 6.1.33
7	Bergen - light - Cantley, 8.1.33
8	Cantley - Gt. Yarmouth, assisting *Tartary*
9	Cantley - molasses - Gt. Yarmouth
	to *Alchymist*
12	Gt. Yarmouth - Cantley, 12.1.33
14	Cantley - molasses - Bergen o Z, 15.1.33
19	Bergen o Z - light - Cantley, 21.1.33
23	Cantley - molasses - Bergen o Z, 24.1.33
25	Bergen o Z - Greenhithe, 27.1.33
30	Greenhithe - spindle oil - Hull, 1.2.33

February
3	Hull - light - Cantley, 5.2.33
6	Cantley - molasses - Bergen o Z, 9.2.33
	towing *Alf Everard.*
10	Bergen o Z - light - Cantley
13	Cantley - molasses - Bergen o Z, 16.2.33
18	Bergen o Z - light - Colchester, 21.2.33
23	Colchester - linseed oil - Erith, 24.2.33
27	Greenhithe - light - Cantley, 28.2.33

March
1	Cantley - molasses - Bergen o Z, 3.3.33
4	Bergen o Z - Greenhithe, 8.3.33
11	Greenhithe - ? - Selby, 12.3.33
13	Selby - PK oil - Purfleet Jetty, 15.3.33
20	Greenhithe - gas oil - Jersey, 25.3.33
26	St.Helier - light - Greenhithe, 27.3.33
29	Purfleet - lube oil - Hull, 31.3.33

April
3	Hull - light - Selby, 4.4.33
4	Selby - cotton seed oil - Silvertown, 7.4.33
8	Coryton - fuel oil - Newhaven, 10.4.33
10	Newhaven - light - Coryton, 11.4.33
11	Coryton - fuel oil - Newhaven, 12.4.33
13	Newhaven - light - Coryton, 13.4.33
17	Greenhithe - fuel oil - Newhaven, 18.4.33
18	Newhaven - light - Coryton, 19.4.33
19	Coryton - fuel oil - Newhaven, 20.4.33
22	Newhaven - light - Greenhithe, 23.4.33
27	Greenhithe - lube oil - Newcastle, 30.4.33

May
1	Newcastle - light - Purfleet, 4.5.33
4	Purfleet - spindle oil - Dundee, 8.5.33
9	Dundee - lube oil - Greenhithe, 12.5.33
16	Greenhithe - light - King's Lynn, 17.5.33
20	King's Lynn - molasses - Ipswich, 21.5.33
22	Ipswich - light - King's Lynn, 23.5.33
24	King's Lynn - molasses - Ipswich, 26.5.33
28	Ipswich - light - King's Lynn, 30.5.33
30	King's Lynn - molasses - Ipswich, 1.6.33

June
2	Ipswich - light - King's Lynn, 3.6.33
7	King's Lynn - molasses - Bergen o Z, 9.6.33
10	Bergen o Z - light - King's Lynn, 12.6.33
13	King's Lynn - molasses - Bergen o Z, 15.6.33
16	Bergen o Z - light - King's Lynn, 17.6.33
18	King's Lynn - molasses - Bergen o Z, 20.6.33
21	Bergen o Z - light - King's Lynn, 22.6.33
25	King's Lynn - molasses - Bergen o Z, 27.6.33
29	Bergen o Z - light - Cantley, 30.6.33

July
1	Cantley - molasses - Bergen o Z, 3.7.33
4	Bergen o Z - Greenhithe (refuel), 5.7.33
5	Greenhithe - Cantley, 7.5.33
9	Cantley - molasses - Bergen o Z, 10.7.33
11	Bergen o Z - light - Cantley, 12.7.33
15	Cantley - molasses - Bergen o Z, 16.7.33
18	Bergen o Z - light - Cantley, 20.8.33
22	Cantley - molasses - Bergen o Z, 23.8.33
24	Bergen o Z - light - King's Lynn, 26.8.33

August
1	King's Lynn - molasses - Bergen o Z, 2.8.33
4	Bergen o Z - Greenhithe (refuel), 5.8.33
5	Greenhithe - Cantley, 7.8.33
9	Cantley - molasses - Bergen o Z, 10.8.33
11	Bergen - light - Cantley, 12.8.33
14	Cantley - molasses - Bergen o Z, 17.8.33

18	Bergen o Z - light - Cantley, 20.8.33
21	Cantley - molasses - Bergen o Z, 23.8.33
24	Bergen o Z - light - King's Lynn, 26.8.33

September

1	King's Lynn - molasses - Bergen o Z, 3.9.33
4	Bergen o Z - Greenhithe, 5.9.33
18	Purfleet - Holehaven, 19.9.33
20	Holehaven - cotton oil - discharge various
30	Coryton - petroleum spirit - Exeter, 2.10.33

October

3	Exeter - light - Northam, 4.10.33
4	Northam - petroleum spirit - Exmouth, 4.10.33
5	Exmouth - light - Coryton, 6.10.33
6	Coryton - petroleum spirit - Woolston, 7.10.33
9	Woolston - light - Cantley, 13.10.33
15	Cantley - molasses - Gt. Yarmouth, 17.10.33 to *Asperity*
18	Gt. Yarmouth - Cantley, 18.10.33 tow *Cambria* and *Ethel Everard*
19	Cantley - molasses - Gt. Yarmouth, 21.10.33 to *Asperity*
22	Gt. Yarmouth - light - Cantley, 22.10.33
24	Cantley - molasses - Gt. Yarmouth, 25.10.33 to *Asperity*
25	Gt. Yarmouth - light - Cantley, 27.10.33
27	Cantley - molasses - Gt. Yarmouth, 29.10.33 to *Asperity*
29	Gt. Yarmouth - light - Cantley, 29.11.33
30	Cantley - molasses - Gt. Yarmouth, 1.11.33 to *Asperity*

November

4	Gt. Yarmouth - light - Selby, 5.11.33
6	Selby - peanut oil - Purfleet Jetty, 8.11.33
13	Greenhithe - light - Cantley, 14.11.33
15	Cantley - molasses - Gt. Yarmouth to *Asperity*
16	Gt. Yarmouth - light - Cantley, 16.11.33
17	Cantley - molasses - Gt. Yarmouth to *Asperity*
19	Gt. Yarmouth - light - Cantley, 20.11.33
21	Cantley - molasses - Gt. Yarmouth, 21.11.33
22	Gt. Yarmouth to search for *Ethel Everard*, but not found - returned Cantley
24	Cantley - molasses - Gt. Yarmouth, 25.11.33 to *Asperity*
26	Gt. Yarmouth - light - Cantley
27	Cantley - molasses - Gt. Yarmouth, 28.11.33 to *Asperity*
28	Cantley - molasses - Gt. Yarmouth, 29.11.33 to *Asperity*

30	Gt. Yarmouth - light - Cantley with *Fred Everard*

December

3	Cantley - molasses - Gt. Yarmouth await ship with *Will Everard*
6	Gt. Yarmouth - light - Cantley
7	Cantley - molasses - Gt. Yarmouth to *Asperity*
8	Gt. Yarmouth - light - Cantley
9	Cantley - molasses - Gt. Yarmouth await ship
13	Gt. Yarmouth - light - Cantley found *Grit* ashore
14	Cantley - molasses - Gt. Yarmouth to *Asperity*
15	Gt. Yarmouth - light - Cantley
19	Cantley - molasses - Cantley, 20.12.33 return with *Alf Everard*
20	Cantley - return with cargo - Gt. Yarmouth await ship
22	Gt. Yarmouth - light - Cantley
23	Cantley - molasses - Gt. Yarmouth to *Asperity*
24	Gt. Yarmouth - light - Cantley
28	Cantley - molasses - Gt. Yarmouth to *Asperity*
29	Gt. Yarmouth - light - Cantley
30	Cantley - molasses - Gt. Yarmouth to *Asperity*
31	Gt. Yarmouth - light - Cantley

1934

January

1	Cantley - molasses - Gt. Yarmouth, 2.1.34 to *Asperity*
3	Gt. Yarmouth - light - Cantley
4	Cantley - molasses - Gt. Yarmouth collision with *River Witham*
5	Gt. Yarmouth - light - Cantley
7	Cantley - molasses - Gt. Yarmouth awaiting ship
12	Gt. Yarmouth - light - Cantley
13	Cantley - molasses - Gt. Yarmouth, 14.1.34 to *Asperity*
15	Cantley - molasses - Gt. Yarmouth to *Asperity*
17	Cantley - molasses - Gt. Yarmouth to *Asperity*
19	Cantley - molasses - Bergen o Z, 22.1.34

22	Bergen o Z - light - Norwich, 23.1.34		**July**	
24	Norwich - light - Cantley, 25.1.34		2	Hull - cotton seed oil - Greenhithe, 4.7.34
	tow *Lady Mary*		4	Greenhithe - cotton seed oil - Silvertown, 5.7.34
26	Cantley - molasses - Bergen o Z, 28.1.34		6	Greenhithe - light - Zaandam, 7.7.34
31	Bergen - light - Cantley, 3.2.34		12	Knollendam - linseed oil - Rotherhithe
February			14	Rotherhithe - light - Zaandam, 15.7.34
5	Cantley - molasses - Bergen o Z, 7.2.34		15	Zaandam - linseed oil - Rotherhithe, 18.7.34
10	Zaandijk - light - Coryton, 11.2.34		20	Greenhithe for repairs
12	Coryton - gas oil - Weymouth, 14.2.34		**August**	
15	Weymouth - light - Greenhithe, 17.2.34		23	Greenhithe - light - Zaandam, 24.8.34
19	Erith - lube oil - Royal Albert Dock, 19.2.34		25	Zaandam - linseed oil - Rotherhithe, 28.8.34
20	Royal Albert Dock - soya bean oil - Erith, 21.2.34		30	Greenhithe - light - Knollendam, 31.8.34
23	Coryton - gas oil - St.Helier, Jersey, 26.2.34		**September**	
March			1	Zaandam - linseed oil - Hull, 5.9.34
1	St.Helier - light - Greenhithe, 2.3.34		6	Hull - light - Zaandam, 8.9.34
6	Greenhithe - light - Zaandam, 8.3.34		8	Zaandam - linseed oil - E. Greenwich, 11.9.34
9	Zaandam - linseed oil - Millwall, 10.3.34		12	Greenhithe - light - Knollendam, 14.9.34
12	Millwall - light - Zaandam, 20.3.34		14	Zaandam - linseed oil - Greenhithe, 15.9.34
15	Zaandam - linseed oil - Rotherhithe, 21.3.34		21	Rotherhithe - light - Knollendam, 22.9.34
24	Purfleet - patching oil - Dundee, 26.3.34		26	Knollendam - linseed oil - Greenhithe, 2.10.34
27	Dundee - light - Hull, 28.3.34		**October**	
31	Hull - soya bean oil - Erith, 2.4.34		3	Rotherhithe - light - Knollendam, 4.10.34
April			4	Knollendam - linseed oil - Rotherhithe, 9.10.34
2	Erith - balance of cargo - Purfleet		11	Rotherhithe - light - Dieppe, 12.10.34
9	Purfleet - lube oil - Hull, 11.4.34		13	Dieppe - linseed oil - Rotherhithe, 14.10.34
13	Hull - light - Zaandam, 16.4.34		17	Rotherhithe - light - Knollendam, 19.10.34
16	Zaandam - linseed oil - Rotherhithe, 18.4.34		20	Zaandam - linseed oil - Hull, 22.10.34
20	Greenhithe - light - Zaandam, 22.4.34		23	Hull - light - Zaandam, 25.10.34
23	Zaandam - linseed oil - Rotherhithe, 28.4.34		25	Zaandam - linseed oil - Greenwich, 27.10.34
May			30	Greenwich - light - Zaandam, 31.10.34
3	Purfleet - lube oil - Hull, 7.5.34		**November**	
8	Hull - light - Knollendam, 10.5.34		1	Zaandam - linseed oil - Greenwich, 4.11.34
11	Knollendam - linseed oil - Greenhihe, 12.5.34		6	Greenhithe - light - Zaandam, 8.11.34
14	Greenhithe - light - Zaandam, 16.5.34		8	Zaandam - linseed oil - Hull, 12.11.34
16	Zaandam - linseed oil - Rotherhithe, 19.5.34		13	Hull - light - Dieppe, 15.11.34
23	Rotherhithe - light - Ipswich, 24.5.34		17	Dieppe - linseed oil - Rotherhithe, 19.11.34
25	Ipswich - linseed oil - Rotherhithe		22	Rotherhithe - light - Knollendam, 24.11.34
28	Rotherhithe - light - Zaandam,1.6.34		25	Zaandam - linseed oil - Millwall, 26.11.34
	tow *Scot*		28	Greenhithe - light - Zaandam, 30.11.34
June			**December**	
1	Zaandam - linseed oil - Rotherhithe, 2.6.34		1	Zaandam - linseed oil - Rotherhithe, 3.12.34
7	Rotherhithe - light - Knollendam		5	Purfleet - gas oil - Lowestoft, 6.12.34
8	Knollendam - linseed oil - Greenwich, 10.6.34		7	Lowestoft - light - Greenhithe, 7.12.34
12	Greenwich - light - Knollendam, 13.6.34		9	Greenhithe - light - Wormerveer, 11.12.34
14	Knollendam - linseed oil - Millwall, 15.6.34		11	Zaandam - linseed oil - Rotherhithe, 13.12.34
18	Millwall - Greenhithe Yard for repairs		17	Purfleet - gas oil - Hull, 19.12.34
21	Purfleet - light - Koog a(an) d(e) Zaan, 23.6.34	20	Hull - light - Gt. Yarmouth, 21.12.34
23	Zaandam - linseed oil - Rotherhithe, 26.6.34		26	Gt. Yarmouth - light - Koog a d Zaan, 27.12.34
29	Greenhithe - light - Hull, 2.7.34		28	Zaandam - linseed oil - Rotherhithe, 31.12.34

1935

January

3	Greenhithe - light - Wormerveer, 4.1.35
5	Zaandam- linseed oil - Hull, 9.1.35
10	Hull - light - Koog a d Zaan, 14.1.35
15	Zaandam - linseed oil - Rotherhithe, 17.1.35
18	Greenhithe - light - Dieppe, 19.1.35
20	Dieppe - linseed oil - Hull, 22.1.35
23	Hull - light - Coryton, 24.1.35
24	Coryton - gas oil - Weymouth, 27.1.35
27	Weymouth - light - Wormerveer, 2.2.35

February

2	Zaandam - linseed oil - Rotherhithe, 5.2.35
7	Greenhithe - light - Zaandam, 10.2.35
11	Zaandam - linseed oil - Millwall, 13.2.35
14	Millwall - light - Knollendam, 16.2.35
17	Zaandam - linseed oil - Hull (Thorne), 25.2.35
27	Hull - light - Wormerveer, 1.3.35

March

2	Zaandam - linseed oil - Hull, 5.2.35
6	Hull - light - Thameshaven, 7.3.35
7	Thameshaven - gas oil - St.Helier, 9.3.35
12	St. Helier - light - Zaandam, 14.3.35
15	Zaandam - linseed oil - Rotherhithe, 18.3.35
19	Greenhithe for repairs
21	Greenhithe - light - Zaandam
22	Zaandam - linseed oil - Hull, 23.3.35
26	Hull - light - Zaandam, 28.3.35
28	Zaandam - linseed oil - Hull, 30.3.35
31	Hull - light - Wormerveer, 1.4.35

April

1	Wormerveer - linseed oil - Hull, 8.4.35
9	Hull - light - Knollendam, 10.4.35
11	Wormerveer - linseed oil - Rotherhithe, 17.4.35
18	Greenhithe for repairs

May

1	Greenhithe - under tow to Doust & Co, Rochester, for repair

September

12	Greenhithe - light - Knollendam, 13.3.35
14	Knollendam - linseed oil - Hull, 16.9.35
21	Hull - load ex. *Alchemist*, oil for Eagle Oil Wharf
23	Hull - light - Wormerveer, 24.9.35
25	Zaandam - linseed oil - Hull, 28.9.35
29	Hull - light - Zwijndrecht, 2.10.35

October

4	Zwijndrecht - linseed oil - Leith, 6.10.35
8	Leith - light - Koog a d Zaan, 13.10.35
14	Zaandam - linseed oil - Rotherhithe, 16.10.35
17	Purfleet - gas oil - Portsmouth, 18.10.35
20	Portsmouth - light - Dieppe, 21.10.35
22	Dieppe - linseed oil - Hull, 24.10.35
26	Hull - light - King's Lynn, 27.10.35
29	King's Lynn - molasses - Ipswich, 31.10.35

November

1	Ipswich - light - King's Lynn, 2.11.35
3	King's Lynn - molasses - Ipswich, 4.11.35
7	Ipswich - light - Greenhithe, 7.11.35
9	Greenhithe - light - King's Lynn, 11.11.35
12	King's Lynn - molasses - Ipswich, 14.11.35
15	Ipswich - light - Cantley, 16.11.35
19	Cantley - molasses - Hammersmith, 20.11.35
22	Hammersmith - light - Cantley, 23.11.35
26	Cantley - molasses - Greenwich, 27.11.35
30	Greenwich - light - Cantley, 1.12.35

December

2	Cantley - molasses - Hammersmith, 4.12.35
6	Hammersmith - light - Cantley, 8.12.35 tow *Will Everard*
10	Cantley - molasses - Hammersmith, 12.12.35
13	Hammersmith - light - Cantley, 16.12.35
18	Cantley - molasses - Hammersmith, 19.12.35
22	Hammersmith - light - Cantley, 24.12.35 tow *Britisher*
28	Cantley - molasses - Vlaardingen, 30.12.35

1936

January

3	Vlaardingen - light - Cantley, 7.1.36
8	Cantley - molasses - Vlaardingen, 13.1.36
16	Vlaardingen - light - Zaandam
17	Zaandam - Linseed oil - Hull, 20.1.36
22	Hull - light - Erith, 23.1.36
23	Erith - cotton seed oil - Purfleet, 25.1.36
27	Purfleet - lube oil - Hull, 30.1.36

February

1	Hull - light - Purfleet, 2.2.36
3	Purfleet - lube oil - Hull, 5.2.36
7	Hull - light - Knollendam, 12.2.36
13	Knollendam - linseed oil - Rotherhithe, 14.2.36
16	Greenhithe - light - Southampton, 18.2.36
19	Northam - linseed oil - Greenwich, 21.2.36
22	Greenwich - light - Zaandam, 23.2.36
24	Zaandam - linseed oil - Rotherhithe, 25.2.36
26	Greenhithe - light - Zaandam, 28.2.36
29	Zaandam - linseed oil - Rotherhithe, 2.3.36

March

6	Purfleet - oils (various) - Newcastle, 9.3.36
10	Newcastle - light - Kattendijk, 13.3.36
14	Kattendijk - linseed oil - Rotherhithe, 16.3.36
19	Purfleet - patching oil - Dundee, 21.3.36
23	Dundee - light - Zaandam, 28.3.36
29	Zaandam - linseed oil - Rotherhithe, 31.3.36

April

1	Rotherhithe - lube oil - Hull, 4.3.36
6	Hull - cotton seed oil - King George V Dock, 8.4.36
	discharged to S.S. *Lochkatrine*
9	Purfleet - gas oil - Portsmouth, 12.4.36
13	Portsmouth - raw cotton oil - Millwall, 17.4.36
	Engine breakdown - towed to Greenhithe
20	Purfleet - gas oil - Poole, 22.4.36
23	Poole - light - Purfleet, 24.4.36
24	Purfleet - gas oil - Poole, 26.4.36
28	Poole - light - Purfleet, 27.4.36
30	Purfleet - gas oil - Poole, 1.5.36

May

2	Poole - batching oil - Dundee
	C.H. Fielder taken ill - entries cease
	Reported ship struck submerged wreckage 11.5.36
	sea water contamination in tanks 3 & 4
15	C.H. Fielder returns to *Prowess*
16	Purfleet - light - Southampton, 17.5.36
18	Southampton - linseed oil - Greenwich, 21.5.36
22	Purfleet - lube oil - Hull, 25.5.36
26	Hull - light - Zaandam, 27.5.36
28	Wormerveer - linseed oil - Rotherhithe, 30.5.36

June

3	Greenhithe - light - Cantley, 4.6.36
5	Cantley - molasses - East Greenwich, 7.6.36
9	Purfleet - light - Cantley, 10.6.36
11	Cantley - molasses - East Greenwich, 12.6.36
13	Greenhithe - light - Cantley, 14.6.36
16	Cantley - molasses - East Greenwich, 17.6.35
18	Greenhithe - light - Cantley, 19.6.36
23	Cantley - molasses - East Greenwich, 24.6.36
25	Greenhithe - light - Cantley, 29.6.36
30	Cantley - molasses - East Greenwich, 1.7.36.

July

2	Greenhithe - light - Cantley, 3.7.36
7	Cantley - molasses - East Greenwich, 8.7.36
10	Greenhithe - light - Cantley, 11.7.36
14	Cantley - molasses - Greenhithe, 15.7.36
22	Greenhithe - lube oil - Hull, 23.7.36
25	Hull - light - Purfleet, 26.7.36
27	Purfleet - gas oil - Oulton Broad, 28.7.36
29	Cantley - molasses - East Greenwich, 2.8.36

August

7	Greenhithe - light - Cantley, 8.8.36
15	Cantley - molasses - East Greenwich, 16.8.36
18	Greenhithe - light - Wormerveer, 20.8.36
21	Knollendam - linseed oil - Hull, 22.8.36
25	Hull - light - Dieppe, 27.8.36
28	Dieppe - linseed oil - Rotherhithe, 29.8.36

September

1	Greenhithe - light - Knollendam, 2.9.36
3	Knollendam - linseed oil - Hull, 5.9.36
8	Hull - light - Knollendam, 9.9.36
10	Knollendam - linseed oil - Hull, 12.9.36
14	Hull - light - East Halton, 14.9.36
16	East Halton - lube oil - Rotherhithe, 18.9.36
21	Greenhithe - light - Wormerveer, 22.9.36
23	Koog a d Zaan - linseed oil - Hull, 28.9.36
29	Hull - light - Koog a d Zaan, 2.10.36

October

3	Koog a d Zaan - linseed oil - Rotherhithe, 5.10.36
6	Rotherhithe - light - Koog a d Zaan, 8.10.36
8	Koog a d Zaan - linseed oil - Rotherhithe, 10.10.36
13	Rotherhithe - light - Wormerveer, 16.10.36
16	Wormerveer - linseed oil - Hull, 24.10.36
28	Hull - light - Koog a d Zaan, 30.10.36
31	Koog a d Zaan - linseed oil - Rotherhithe, 2.11.36

November

4	Greenhithe - light - Wormerveer, 5.11.36
6	Zaandam - linseed oil - Rotherhithe, 14.11.36
18	Rotherhithe - light - Zaandam, 22.11.36
23	Zaandam - linseed oil - Rotherhithe, 26.11.36
27	Greenhithe - light - Koog a d Zaan, 28.11.36
30	Koog a d Zaan - linseed oil - Rotherhithe,11.12.36

December

12	Greenhithe - light - Wormerveer, 14.12.36
15	Wormerveer - linseed oil - Hull, 22.12.36
24	Hull - light - Zaandam, 28.12..36
29	Zaandam - linseed oil - Rotherhithe, 31.12.36

1937

January

2	Greenhithe - light - Antwerp, 3.1.37
4	Antwerp - linseed oil - Rotherhithe, 9.1.37
13	Greenhithe - light - Antwerp, 14.1.37
15	Antwerp - linseed oil - Rotherhithe, 17.1.37
22	Greenhithe - light - Kattendijk, 25.1.37
27	Antwerp - linseed oil - Hull, 1.2.37

February

3	Hull - soya bean oil - Erith, 5.2.37
	to Greenhithe for repairs and survey
	Injury to C.H. Fielder

March

	C.H. Fielder to S.B. *Her Majesty* as Master
12	Greenhithe - light - Wormerveer, 15.3.37
17	Knollendam - linseed oil - Greenhithe, 19.3.37
	C.H. Fielder to M.V. *Prowess* as Master
24	Greenhithe - light - Knollendam, 25.3.37
26	Knollendam - linseed oil - Rotherhithe, 29.3.37
31	Greenhithe - light - Wormerveer, 2.4.37

April

3	Wormerveer - linseed oil - Rotherhithe, 4.4.37
6	Rotherhithe - light - Knollendam, 7.4.37
8	Knollendam - linseed oil - Rotherhithe, 10.4.37
13	Greenhithe - light - Wormerveer, 15.4.37
16	Zaandam - linseed oil - Rotherhithe, 18.4.37
21	Greenhithe - light - Knollendam, 23.4.37
24	Zaandam - linseed oil - Rotherhithe, 28.4.37
30	Rotherhithe - light - Knollendam, 1.5.37

May

2	Zaandam - linseed oil - Rotherhithe, 2.5.37
5	Rotherhithe - light - Wormerveer, 7.5.37
7	Zaandam - linseed oil - Rotherhithe, 10.5.37
11	Rotherhithe - light - Zaandam, 12.5.37
12	Zaandam - linseed oil - Hull, 14.5.37
15	Hull - soya bean oil - Erith, 17.5.37
18	Greenhithe - light - Knollendam, 20.5.37
21	Zaandam - linseed oil - Rotherhithe, 23.5.37
26	Greenhithe - light - Wormerveer, 27.5.37
27	Wormerveer - linseed oil - Rotherhithe, 29.5.37

June

1	Purfleet - lube oil - Hull, 3.6.37
5	Hull - light - Zaandam, 6.6.37
7	Zaandam - linseed oil - Rotherhithe, 8.6.37
10	Greenhithe - light - Zaandam, 12.6.37
12	Zaandam - linseed oil - Rotherhithe, 13.6.37
16	Greenhithe - light - Wormerveer, 17.6.37
18	Wormerveer - linseed oil - Rotherhithe, 20.6.37
23	Rotherhithe - light - Koog a d Zaan, 24.6.37
25	Koog a d Zaan - linseed oil - Millwall, 26.6.37
29	*Prowess* to Greenhithe shipyard for repairs

July

3	Greenhithe - trials - Wormerveer, 5.7.37
6	Zaandam - linseed oil - Hull, 8.7.37
9	Hull - light - Amsterdam, 10.7.37
12	Amsterdam - linseed oil - Rotherhithe, 14.7.37
15	Greenhithe - light - Antwerp, 17.7.37
20	Antwerp - linseed oil - Rotherhithe, 21.7.37
24	Greenhithe - light - Koog a d Zaan, 25.7.37
26	Koog a d Zaan - linseed oil - Hull, 28.7.37
29	Hull - light - Wormerveer, 31.7.37

August

2	Wormerveer - linseed oil - Rotherhithe, 3.8.37
6	Greenhithe - light - Knollendam, 9.8.37
9	Knollendam - linseed oil - Hull, 11.8.37
12	Hull - light - Amsterdam, 14.8.37
16	Amsterdam - linseed oil - Rotherhithe, 18.8.37
20	Greenhithe - light - Zaandam, 23.8.37
24	Zaandam - linseed oil - Hull, 26.8.37
27	Hull - light - Knollendam, 30.8.37
30	Knollendam - linseed oil - Rotherhithe, 2.9.37

September

4	Greenhithe - light - Wormerveer, 6.9.37
8	Zaandam - Linseed oil - Hull, 14.9.37
17	Hull - light - Wormerveer, 20.9.37
20	Zaandam - linseed oil - Rotherhithe, 23.9.37
24	Greenhithe - light - Selby, 26.9.37
27	Selby - ground nut oil - Silvertown, 29.9.37
	C.H. Fielder leaves *Prowess* following death of his wife

October

	C.H. Fielder rejoins *Prowess* in Hull on 15/10/37
16	Hull - light - Antwerp, 18.10.37
20	Antwerp - linseed oil - Rotherhithe, 22.10.37
23	Greenhithe - light - Antwerp, 27.10.37
28	Antwerp - linseed oil - Rotherhithe, 29.10.37
30	Rotherhithe - light - Zaandam, 1.11.37

November

1	Zaandam - linseed oil - Hull, 3.11.37
4	Hull - pella oil - Millwall, 8.11.37
8	Greenhithe - light - Zaandam, 15.11.37
15	Zaandam - linseed oil - Hull, 17.11.37
20	Hull - light - Wormerveer, 23.11.37
24	Wormerveer - linseed oil - Hull, 27.11.37

December

1	Hull - washed cotton oil - Purfleet, 3.12.37
7	Greenhithe - light - Wormerveer, 9.12.37
10	Zaandam - linseed oil - Hull, 16.12.37
18	Hull - light - Wormerveer, 20.12.37
21	Wormerveer - linseed oil - Rotherhithe, 23.12.37
27	Greenhithe - light - Wormerveer, 28.12.37
29	Zaandam - linseed oil - at anchor, 31.12.37
	C.H. Fielder leaves *Prowess* and F.T. Everard & Sons Ltd.

Details of vessels, where known, which occur in the text.

Name:
Propulsion,
Type;
Official Number;
when built;
ownership when
referred to in narrative;
fate.

Particulars of Vessels aboard which Charlie Fielder served shown in **bold** type and with additional data.

Acclivity: Motor, tanker; O.N.162667; built 1931; owned Everard; sank 1952.

Activity: Motor, dry cargo; O.N.162654; built 1931; owned Everard; continued existence doubtful, deleted from Lloyds Register 1990.

Actuosity: **Motor, dry cargo; O.N.163316; built 1933 by George Brown & Co., Garvel Shipyard, Greenock, Yard No.183, for F.T. Everard & Sons Ltd., Greenhithe; 359grt, 177nrt; dimensions 135.3 x 24.6 x 9.1 feet; 5 cyl. 2SA oil engine by Newbury Diesel Co. Ltd., Newbury; sank off Cromer 3.10.40 after striking submerged object whilst bound Newcastle to London with wheat.**

Affirmity: Motor, tanker; O.N.185983; built 1928; owned Everard; broken-up 1964.

Agility: **Steam, tanker; O.N.147633; built 1924 by George Brown & Co., Garvel Shipyard, Greenock, Yard No.141, for F.T. Everard & Sons Ltd., Greenhithe; 522grt, 183nrt; dimensions 160.3 x 26.2 x 12.3 feet; triple expansion steam engine by Wm. Beardmore & Co. Ltd., Coatbridge; first of many vessels built for Everard by George Brown; sold to BISCO, broken-up by T.W. Ward Ltd. at Grays, Essex, 1958.**

Agnes Mary: **Sprits'l sailing barge; O.N.89870; built 1894 by William Felton at Sandwich, Kent, for William Waters Tritton and others; registered at Faversham; 65grt, 55nrt; dimensions 81.5 x 18.6 x 5.4 ft; acquired by Alice Everard 1919; broken-up at Greenhithe 1953.**

Alchymist: Steam, tanker; O.N.105770; built 1895; owned Everard; broken-up 1950.

Alert: Sprits'l sailing barge; O.N.63664; built 1870; owned Everard; broken-up 1929.

Alf Everard: Sprits'l 'mulie' sailing barge/converted to motor coaster 1943; O.N.148691; built 1925; owned Everard; sunk in collision 1953.

Alfred: Sprits'l sailing barge; O.N.79863; built 1878; owned George Eales; Register closed 1940, fate uncertain.

Amenity: **Motor, dry cargo; O.N.160543; built 1928 by Fellows & Co. Ltd., Gt. Yarmouth, for F.T. Everard & Sons. Ltd., Greenhithe; 262grt, 125nrt; dimensions 115.1 x 23.2 x 8.7 feet; with 5 cyl. 2SA P50 type oil engine by Plenty & Son Ltd., Newbury; lengthened to 135.2 ft. and re-engined 3 cyl. 2SA SBD type oil engine by Newbury Diesel Co. Ltd., Newbury 1936; Struck a mine on 15.11.1940 while bound Goole to Margate with coal, subsequently sunk by gunfire.**

Annuity: Motor, dry cargo; O.N.139195; built 1916; owned Everard; broken-up 1960.

Apexity: Steam, tanker; O.N.185895; built 1945; owned Everard; broken-up 1975.

Apricity: Motor, dry cargo O.N.163393; built 1933; owned Everard; continued existence doubtful, deleted from Lloyds Register 1993.

Aptity: Motor, tanker; O.N.167204; built 1939; owned Everard; broken-up 1987.

Archibald Russell: 4-masted sailing vessel, dry cargo; O.N.121209; built 1905; owned Gustaf Erikson, Mariehemn; broken-up 1949.

Aridity: Motor, dry cargo; O.N.162607; built 1931; owned Everard; fate unknown since 1976.

Aseity: Motor, dry cargo; O.N.163574; built 1935; owned Everard; continued existence doubtful, deleted from Lloyds Register 2000.

Asian: Hulk, Weymouth Bay; no data located.

Asperity: Steam, tanker; O.N.161300; built 1929; owned Everard; sunk 1941, torpedoed by German E-boat.

Assiduity; Motor, dry cargo; O.N.162508; built 1930; owned Everard; broken-up 1961.

Assurity: Motor, barge; O.N.146049; built 1921; owned Everard; broken-up 1959.

Attunity: Steam, tanker; O.N.185896; built 1945; owned Everard; broken-up 2001.

Audacity: Steam, tanker; O.N.148704; Built 1925 by George Brown & Co. Ltd., Garvel Shipyard, Greenock, Yard No.149, for F.T. Everard & Sons Ltd., Greenhithe; 589grt, 242nrt; dimensions 172.8 x 26.7 x 12.7 feet; triple expansion steam engine by Wm. Beardmore, Coatbridge; sunk by mine south of the Humber Lightvessel 1.3.1942, whilst bound Selby to Purfleet with palm kernel oil.

Authority: Steam, tanker; O.N.160484; built1928; owned Everard; broken-up 1966.

Azurity: Motor, tanker; O.N.185868; built 1949; owned Everard; broken-up 1965.

Beaulieu: Steam, tug; O.N.114536; built 1901; owned Edward T. Agius Co., Southampton; broken-up 1950.

Bellavale: Steam, dry cargo; O.N.129630; built 1910; owned Everard; broken-up 1956.

Bessie: Dumb, dry cargo barge.

Betty Hudson: Motor, barge, ex. Admiralty X-Lighter X081; O.N.148503; built 1915; owned B.W.Steamship, Tug & Lighter Co. Ltd. and W. Scott; last reported, engines removed, at Queenborough, Kent, 2005; survival uncertain.

Black Duck: Sprits'l sailing barge; O.N.86983; built 1882 by John Bazeley White at Black Duck Wharf, Swanscombe, for their family account; 58 tons; dimensions 82.6 x 19.0 x 5.9 feet; owned Associated Portland Cement Manufacturers (A.P.C.M.) 1901, sold in June 1932 to The Thames Transport Co. (already de-rigged) for £40.

Brent: Open dumb dry cargo barge; P.L.A. Barge No.12492.

Britisher: Sprits'l sailing barge; O.N.115802, built 1902 by F.T. Everard, Greenhithe, for own account; 95grt, 68nrt; dimensions 87.0 x 22.2 x 6.9 ft.; sunk by mine off Maplin Sands 4.11.1941, with loss of all hands, when bound Gt. Yarmouth to London.

Briton: Sprits'l sailing barge; O.N.114752, built 1901 by F.T. Everard, Greenhithe, for W.T. Clifford, acquired by Everard 1910, 82grt, 65nrt; dimensions 85.0 x 21.2 x 6.4 ft.; driven ashore in heavy weather and wrecked near Blakeney, Norfolk 20.12.1923, when bound Boston, Lincs, to Sandwich, Kent.

Cambria: Sprits'l 'mulie' sailing barge; O.N.120676; built 1906 by F.T. Everard, Greenhithe, for own account; restored by charitable trust and still under sail 2014, on National Historic Ships register.

Capable: Auxiliary schooner/later converted to motor coaster; O.N.144446; built 1918, owned Everard; mined and sank 1940.

Capacitas: Steam, tanker; Italian; built 1918; owned Societe An. Mare Nostrum, Genoa; Torpedoed and sunk 1941.

Cecil: Sprits'l sailing barge; O.N.118217; built 1905; owned Sankey & Co. Ltd.; broken-up after collision 1932.

Ceres, H.M.S.: Steam, C Class Light Cruiser; built 1917; broken-up 1946.

Charlight: Motor, canal tug; P.L.A. No.697; built 1936; owned Charrington, Gardner, Lockett (London) Ltd.; preserved and operational 2014, on National Historic Ships register.

Charlock: Steam, river tug; O.N.160589; built 1928; owned Charrington, Gardner, Lockett (London) Ltd.; broken-up 1963.

Chessington: Motor, dry-cargo (collier); O.N.180851; built 1946; owned Wandsworth & District Gas Co.; converted to storage hulk, Gothenberg 1966, fate unknown.

Clan Monroe: Steam, dry cargo, O.N.141882; built 1918; owned Clan Line Steamers Ltd.; mined and sank 1940.

Classic: Tank dumb barge.

Co-operator: Motor, tug/tender; O.N.133430; built 1913; owned Everard; houseboat by 1985.

Compass: Tank dumb barge.

Cowl: Tank dumb barge.

Crow: Sprits'l sailing barge; O.N.101911; built 1891; owned Sales; broken-up 1948.

Dart: Open dumb dry cargo barge; P.L.A. Barge No. 13237.

Despatch: Sprits'l sailing barge; O.N.73607; built 1876; owned Everard; broken-up 1920.

Diamond: Dumb barge fitted with tanks; owned Everard.

Dogwatch: Tank dumb barge; owned Everard.

Eastward: Tank dumb barge; owned Everard.

Elizabeth: Sprits'l sailing barge; O.N.77023; built 1877; owned Everard; broken-up 1924.

Emerald: Dumb barge fitted with tanks; owned Everard.

Energy: Sprits'l sailing barge; O.N.56870; built 1867; owned Everard; broken-up after collision and sinking 1903.

Ethel Everard: Sprits'l 'mulie' sailing barge; O.N.149723; built 1926; owned Everard; abandoned Dunkirk 1940, total loss.

Fairy: Steam, tug; (possibly) O.N.93655; built 1902; East Coast Steam Ship Co. Ltd.; out of MNL by 1939.

Faverolle: Steam, tug; O.N.144564; built 1919; owned Everard; broken-up 1938.

Frank M: Motor, tanker; O.N.161309; built 1929; owned T.J. Metcalf; broken up 1964.

Frank Pink: Motor, dry cargo; ex. Admiralty X-Lighter X71; O.N.147995; built 1915; owned Everard; broken-up 1948.

Fred Everard: Sprits'l 'mulie' sailing barge/converted to motor coaster 1938; O.N.149743; built 1926; owned Everard; sank in collision 1956.

Gerty: Sprits'l 'swimmie' sailing barge; O.N.108259; built 1897; owned Everard; caught fire, sank, raised and broken-up 1933.

Glenogle: Motor, dry cargo; O.N.144217; built 1920; owned Glen Line; broken-up (as Blue Funnel *Deucalion*) 1956.

Graphic: Sprits'l sailing barge; O.N.74807; built 1876; owned Wm. Lee, Son & Co. Ltd.; hulked 1914.

Gravelines III: Ketch rigged sailing barge; O.N.88824; built 1891; owned Mrs. S. Bailey; wrecked 1924.

Greenhithe: Sprits'l 'mulie' sailing barge; O.N.147562; built 1923; owned Everard; broken-up 1963.

Grit: Auxiliary motor ketch barge; O.N.135249; built 1913, owned Everard; sunk by U-boat gunfire 1916.

Grit (2): Motor, dry cargo; O.N.147531; built 1923; owned Everard; sank in collision 1934.

H. Pierrepoint: **Sprits'l sailing barge; O.N.84415; built 1881 by Curel at Frindsbury, Kent, for T. Banks; registered at Rochester; 45t; owned by her builder in 1883, sold to Honey in 1889, sold to George Eales in 1896, sold on Eales death to Jack Rayfield, Northfleet, sold to Smy in 1919; lost in the Spitway, Thames Estuary on 26/04/19 when loaded with pyrites.**

Harriot: Schooner; Not on Register, possibly that built by Cliffe at Knottingly; wrecked when collided with Sunderland pierhead 1901.

Heather Pet: see *Assurity*.

Helena: Motor, not identified.

Her Majesty: **Sprits'l sailing barge; O.N.109106; built 1897 by White, Sittingbourne, for Margate Hoy Co.; registered at Ramsgate; 62grt, 53nrt; dimensions 82.0 x 18.7 x 5.7 feet; acquired Wm.J. Everard 1918, sold as houseboat 1947; broken-up.**

Hibernia: Sprits'l 'mulie' sailing barge; O.N.120677; built 1906; owned Everard; driven ashore and wrecked 1937.

Hilda: **Sprits'l sailing barge; O.N.87054; built 1881 by Robert Webb, Henley-on-Thames for John Bazeley White & Bros. Ltd.; registered at London; 72grt, 72nrt; dimensions 83.0 x 17.0 x 6.0 feet; sold to Associated Portland Cement Manufacturers (1900) Ltd. in 1900; acquired by F.T. Everard in December 1902; broken up December 1934.**

Industry: Sprits'l sailing barge; O.N.54763; built 1866; owned Everard; broken-up 1912.

Inward: Tank dumb barge; owned Everard.

Irishman (possibly): Steam, screw tug; O.N.160827; built 1929; owned United Towing Co. Ltd.; broken-up 1986.

J.M.W.: Sprits'l sailing barge; O.N.84417; built 1881 by A. White, Blackwall for Robins & Co; registered at London; 44 tons; sold to London Lighterage Co., sold to A.P.C.M., sold to Harrison in 1932; derelict at Conyer, Kent by 1937; broken-up 1950.

John Bayly: Sprits'l sailing barge; O.N.104760; built 1895; owned Everard; broken-up 1937.

King Edward VII: Steam, paddle tug; O.N.111083; built 1901, owned Ridley Steam Tug Co. Ltd.; broken-up 1950.

Lady Marjorie: Sprits'l sailing barge; O.N.102783; built 1893, owned Everard; housebarge Penryn, derelict 1980s.

Lady Martin: Steam, dry cargo; O.N.133548; built 1913; owned British & Irish Steam Packet Co., Dublin; sunk by air raid in Baltic Sea 1941.

Lady Mary: Sprits'l sailing barge; O.N.112692; built 1900; owned Everard; hulked Erith 1967.

Lady Maud: Sprits'l sailing barge; O.N.118305; built 1903; owned Everard; broken-up 1959.

Lea: Open dumb dry cargo barge; P.L.A. Barge No. 12491.

Leeward: Tank dumb barge; owned Everard.

Lochkatrine: Motor, dry cargo; O.N.146228; built 1922; owned Royal Mail Lines Ltd.; torpedoed and sunk 1942.

Lord Kitchener: Sprits'l sailing barge; O.N.110073; built 1899; owned Everard; wrecked off Dartmouth 1926.

Mahout: Steam, dry cargo; O.N.147347; built 1925, owned T. & J. Brocklebank; broken-up 1961.

Margaret Lockett, later *P.B. Everard*: Motor, river tug; O.N.184562; built 1952; owned Charrington, Gardner, Lockett (London) Ltd.; believed broken-up 1990.

Martha: Sprits'l sailing barge: O.N.106530; built 1897; owned Everard; driven ashore and wrecked 1941.

Martinet: Ketch rigged 'boomie' sailing barge; O.N.128880; built 1912; owned Everard; sank 1941.

Mary Graham: Sprits'l sailing barge; O.N.127261; built 1913; owned Everard; driven ashore and wrecked 1937.

Middlewatch: Tank dumb barge; owned Everard.

Morningwatch: Tank dumb barge; owned Everard.

Mystery: **Ketch rigged 'boomie' sailing barge; O.N.21364; built 1865 for R., W. & J. Lewis; registered at Harwich, later Rochester; 64 tons; dimensions 82.5 x 18.5 x 6.3 feet; sold to W.H. Bensted 1874; sold to Charles Tuff Jnr. 1886; sold to C. Tuff Jnr., G.W. Gill & F. Miskin 1886; sold to C. Tuff Jnr., F. Miskin, G.W.Gill Jnr., J.E. Gill, E. Gill, E.A. Gill & H. Browne 1888; sold to Mary A. Tuff, C. Tuff Jnr. & F. Miskin 1889; sold to C. Tuff Jnr. & Augustus A. Arnold 1897; sold to Samuel West 1902, sold to T. Langford 1920; sold to A.W. Claringbold & L.J.**

Ballands 1923; sold to A.W. Claringbold 1923; sold to F.S. Riding 1929; broken-up c.1938.

Nightwatch: Tank dumb barge; owned Everard.

Nitrogen: Tank dumb barge.

Norseman: Steam, dry cargo; O.N.119150; built 1904; owned Everard; sank following collision 1925.

Northward: Tank dumb barge; owned Everard.

Olnal: Steam, tanker; O.N.146149; built 1921; owned Admiralty; fate unknown.

Olympia: Ketch rigged 'boomie' sailing barge; O.N.114453; built 1902; owned Samuel West; run down and sunk 1918.

Orcades: Steam-turbine, passenger ship; O.N.165501; built 1937; owned Orient Steam Navigation Co. Ltd.; torpedoed and sunk 1942.

Otterhound: Steam, tanker; O.N.149879; built 1932; owned Coastal Tankers Ltd.; sank 1960.

Outward: Tank dumb barge; owned Everard.

P.B. Everard (see *Margaret Lockett*)

Pearl: Dumb barge fitted with tanks; owned Everard.

Pembury: Dumb barge, P.L.A. No.17768; built c.1955; owned Charrington, Gardner, Lockett (London) Ltd.; fate unknown.

Port Hunter: Steam-turbine, cargo ship; O.N.146641; built 1922; owned Commonwealth & Dominion Line Ltd. (Port Line); torpedoed and sunk 1942.

Portwatch: Tank dumb barge; owned Everard.

Pride of the Colne: Sprits'l sailing barge; O.N.58170; built 1869; owned Everard; broken-up 1924.

Prompt: Sprits'l sailing barge; O.N.73743; built 1876; owned Everard; broken-up 1922.

Prowess: **Motor, tanker; O.N.149707; built 1926 by George Brown & Co. Ltd., Greenock (Yard No. 154), for F.T. Everard & Sons Ltd., registered at London, No.114 in 1926; 207grt, 77nrt; 106.1 x 23.2 x 9.1 feet; 200 bhp 4 Cyl. 2SA 'P50' type oil engine by Plenty & Son Ltd, Newbury, built under License to a 1910 design by Kromhout of Rotterdam; one mast rigged smack; Lloyds Register supplement +100A1 at Lloyds, machinery aft, Q 33' - F 14' - 104'3" x 23'0" x 9'0", 7 BH [bulkheads], FPT [fore-peak tank] 8 tons, APT [aft-peak tank] 18 tons - coils - summer freeboard 7$^{1}/_{2}$".**

Re-engined with 4 Cyl. 2SA 'F' type oil engine by Newbury Diesel Co. Ltd. in 1938.

P.L.A. Owners No.1771, Barge Register No.17687, Tomage 77 m 128 b, length 106$^{1}/_{10}$ x 28$^{2}/_{10}$ x 9 feet.

Sold to A.E. Peirce, Canvey Island, 1961; resold to N.V. Machine & Scheepsloperij 'De Koophandel', Nieuw Lekkerland, The Netherlands, for breaking. Broken up 1962.

Pudge: Sprits'l sailing barge; O.N.127274; built 1922; owned The London & Rochester Trading Co. Ltd. maintained by Thames Sailing Barge Trust and still under sail 2014.

Ramble: Motor, tanker, ex. Admiralty X-Lighter X161; O.N.148606; built 1915; owned Everard; broken-up 1959.

Ramilles, H.M.S.: Steam turbine, Revenge Class battleship, built 1916; broken-up 1949.

Regent: Motor, canal tug; built 1952; owned Charrington, Gardner, Lockett (London) Ltd.; fate unknown.

Renown: Sprits'l sailing barge; O.N.55183; built 1866; owned Samuel L. Smith, Halling, from 1883 (N.B. built by Wm. Lee of Halling, owned by Lee 1904); Register closed 1927.

Revenge: Lighter.

River Witham: Motor, dry cargo; O.N.147476; built 1914; owned R. Hunt, Hull; wrecked Humber Estuary 1945.

Roam: Motor, tanker, ex. Admiralty X-Lighter X161; O.N.145222; built 1915; owned Everard; sank 1926.

Rover: Steam, tug; not identified.

Royalty: Sprits'l 'mulie' sailing barge; O.N.1109919; built 1898; owned Everard; beached and abandoned Dunkirk 1940, total loss.

Ruby: Dumb barge fitted with tanks; owned Everard.

Sandwich: Steam, tug; O.N.97708; built 1892; owned B. Jacob & Son Ltd.; broken-up 1936.

Sapphire: Dumb barge fitted with tanks; owned Everard.

Sara: Sprits'l sailing barge; O.N.115858; built 1902; owned Everard; broken-up 1964.

Saunter: Motor, tanker, ex. Admiralty X-Lighter X106; O.N.146604; built 1915; owned Everard; broken-up 1970.

Scot: Sprits'l sailing barge; O.N.112845; built 1901; owned Everard; broken-up 1964.

Sedulity: Motor, dry cargo; O.N.164663; built 1936; owned Everard; broken-up 1981.

Snipe: Sprits'l sailing barge; O.N.90983; built 1886; owned George Eales, Greenhithe; run down and sunk 1932, wreck blown up.

Southward: Tank dumb barge; owned Everard.

Stanley Baldwin: Motor, dry cargo, ex. Admiralty X-Lighter X167; O.N.148506; built 1915; owned Everard; believed broken-up 1985.

Starboardwatch: Tank dumb barge; owned Everard.

Stonebow: Motor, tug/tender; O.N.136716; built 1913; owned Everard; broken-up 1953.

Tactful: Steam, tug; O.N.126716; built 1909; owned Gt. Yarmouth Steam Tug Co. Ltd.; broken-up 1964.

Tarn: Dumb barge, P.L.A. No.17583; built c.1954; owned Charrington, Gardner, Lockett (London) Ltd.; fate unknown.

Tartary: Steam, tanker; O.N.147548; built 1923; owned Everard; sank 1938.

Thistle: Sailing bawley: Fishing No.RR2 (Rochester, Kent); built 1887; owned Fielder; restored and still in commission, 2014.

Thorne: Sailing Humber keel; no information found.

Tiff: Dumb barge, P.L.A. No.17549; built c.1953; owned Charrington, Gardner, Lockett (London) Ltd.; fate unknown.

Tirydail: Steam, dry cargo; O.N.136149; built 1918 by C.H. Walker & Co. Ltd., Sudbrook, Yard No.231, for Cleeves Western Valleys

Anthracite Collieries Ltd, Swansea; 650grt, 393nrt; dimensions 176.0 x 27.6 x 11.8 feet; Triple expansion steam engine by Plenty & Son Ltd., Newbury; acquired by F.T. Everard & Sons Ltd. in 1926, sold to Williamstown Shipping Co. Ltd., London and renamed *Lincolnbrook* 2.1946; sold to Duff, Herbert & Mitchell Ltd., London and renamed *Joseph Mitchell* 7.1957; sank off Ballycotton, Ireland, after striking submerged rocks, whist on passage Garston to Cork with coal, 9.2.1950.

Tope: Dumb barge, P.L.A. No.17548; built c.1953; owned Charrington, Gardner, Lockett (London) Ltd.; fate unknown.

Tosca: **Steam, dry cargo; O.N.99738; built 1908 by Ailsa Shipbuilding Co. Ltd., Ayr, Yard No.208, for Mrs G.A. Smith, Glasgow; 449grt, 169nrt; dimensions 155.4 x 25.6 x 12.5 feet, 2-cyl. compound steam engine by Ailsa Shipbuilding Co. Ltd., Troon; acquired by F.T. Eberhardt 10.1916; Sold to W.A. Wilson, Southampton 9.1926;; sold to G.B. Figari, Antonio Maggiola & Co., Genoa, 12.1933; Sold to G.M. Scotto, Genoa, 1940; torpedoed and sunk by H.M. Submarine Sahib south of Lipari.**

Troy: Dumb barge, P.L.A. No.17584; built c.1954; owned Charrington, Gardner, Lockett (London) Ltd.; fate unknown.

Umeälv, ex. *Hansa*, ex, *Nordfold*: Steam, O.N.3007446; built 1917; registered Hamburg; owned August Bolten, Wm. Miller's Successors; sunk by aircraft 1944, raised and broken-up 1947.

Upward: Tank dumb barge; owned Everard.

Velocity: Dumb barge.

Veronica: Sprits'l sailing barge; O.N.120691; built 1906; owned Everard; hulked 1976.

Victoria: Dumb tank barge.

Viola: Sprits'l sailing barge; O.N.110980; built 1900; owned Sankey & Co. Ltd.; Register closed 1934, derelict 1941, broken-up.

Wander: Motor, tanker, ex. Admiralty X-Lighter X3; O.N.146683; built 1915; owned Everard; sank 1928.

Westward: Tank dumb barge; owned Everard.

Will Everard: Sprits'l 'mulie' sailing barge; O.N.148677; built 1925; owned Everard; still in service as hospitality charter vessel 2014.

William: Sprits'l sailing barge; O.N.67035; built 1872; owned George B. Livingstone, Harry Timms, Alexander Reid & George Eales (Managing Owner); broken-up 1919.

Willie: Sprits'l sailing barge; O.N.81854, built 1879; owned William G.M. Sankey; converted to lighter 1934, fate unknown.

Windward: Tank dumb barge; owned Everard.

Worcester, ex. H.M.S. *Frederick William*: built 1860; owned by Thames Nautical Training College; broken up 1948-1953.

Yantlet: Steam, salvage vessel; O.N.147478, built 1916, owned Port of London Authority; broken-up 1955.

Ytirussa: see *Assurity*.

The Fielder Archive comprises the items scheduled in this Appendices.

The Fielder Archive has been lodged with various organisations. The letters in parenthesis after each item indicate where.
NMM = National Maritime Museum, Object Cat. No. REG09/000151.
TUC = Trades Union Congress.
SSBR = Society for Sailing Barge Research Archive.
H&F = Hammersmith & Fulham Library.

1   Identity card, 29.iv.43   AJA 1138190   Charles H. Fielder, 73,Riverside Gardens, Hammersmith. [NMM]

2   Quarto Exercise Book (red paper cover):

    2.a   Diary of the S.S.*Tosca* 23.4.1924   (loading Rochester to Middlesbrough) to 23rd April to Tyne & Tees - includes notes on Millwall Docks etc., - address book. [NMM]

    2.b   Insert, Log of the M.V. *Amenity* C.H.Fielder, Mate joined Wednesday 17th October 1928 at Swanscombe Buoys to Dungeness. [NMM]

    2.c   Letter 20.1.24 from S.S. *Tosca* at Great Yarmouth to Fielder from J. MacDonald (Tosca refit, new windlass, propellers, lining). [NMM]

3   Chief Officer's Log Book of the *Prowess*.
Capt. J.Brown, 1 Sept.1926, Greenock to Greenhithe; subsequently W. Coker, Ipswich to Antwerp. [NMM]
Items found in log:

    3.a   F.T. Everard & Sons Ltd. delivery note, 200 ton washed cotton oil for London. [NMM]

    3.b   F.T. Everard & Sons Ltd. letter, 30.6.37, warning of piling works of R. Yare. [NMM]

    3.c   Office of Receiver of Wreck 6.9.37, casualty return re. machinery damage, put back to Ijmuiden, 30.8.37. [NMM]

    3.d   F.T. Everard & Sons Ltd. letter, delivery note 210,000 kilos raw Dutch linseed oil in bulk to Hull August 1937. [NMM]

    3.e   F.T. Everard & Sons Ltd. delivery note 210.000 kilos raw Dutch linseed oil for Hull, duplicate. [NMM]

    3.f   J. Dennis & Co. Ltd. letter, 25.10.37 to Capt.Fielder, S.S. *Prowess* [sic.] re. Dennis Portable Combined Radio Direction Finder, £19.19.0. [NMM]

    3.g   Delivery note, Pella oil, from John L.Seaton & Co.Ltd. Hull. [NMM]

    3.h   F.T. Everard & Sons Ltd. letter, 28.12.37 re. pension scheme for officers. [NMM]

    3.i.   **(i)**   T.J. Metcalf letter, 25.1.1938, confirming temporary appointment as captain of M.V. *Frank M.* [NMM]

        (ii)   J.R. Wood & Co., cc. letter 2.2.38, change of orders. [NMM]

        (iii)   T.J. Metcalf letter, 4.2.38, orders for Northam, Southampton to load Fawley. [NMM]

        (iv)   Letter to Capt. C. Fielder, M.V. *Frank M*, from T.J. Metcalf, 9.2.1938 (Capt. Mann now fit for work at Purfleet). [NMM]

    3.j   London Port Emergency Committee P.L.A., letter, 15.6.1942, Special Temporary Naval Service. [NMM]

4   Boots scribbling diaries, 1933 - 1934 - 1935 - 1936 - 1937 (draft log(?), daily log books M.V. *Prowess* beam 23-3, Height from bottom to wheelhouse 26.6; from poop to wheelhouse 14.3; beam 23.4; height 26.9; poop to wheelhouse 14.3. [NMM]

5   The Pilots Guide for the English Channel, 1918, with numerous charts and plans of harbours, 232pp + index   (5¹/₂" x 9").

6   Guide to the Northsea-Canal and the harbours of Ijmuiden & Amsterdam for 1936. English text, 131pp + advertisements 12pp, with chart, diagrams etc. (No cover).

7	Tide, Distance & Speed Tables, 1941, Henry Hughes & Son, 271pp, Blue cover (3"x4½").
8	Rough Goods Lighterage Trade, Working Agreement and Rates of Pay, 1948; Foolscap draft Agreement between Master Lightermen etc., Union and T & G.W. [TUC]
9	Offprint from publication 'Blood Red Roses, the supply of Merchant Seamen in the 19th Century', by Stephen Jones pps.429-442 from publication.. [TUC]
10	Offprint from Maritime History, Vol. 3 No.1, April 1973, pps.35-118; Community and Organisation, Early Seamen's Trade Unionism on the North East Coast, 1768 - 1844, by Stephen Jones.. [TUC]
11	Building a Greater Britain, We lead the World, by Michael Foot; Co-Op Press newspaper election address (Hammersmith, Tom Williams). [H&F]
12	Spritsail, Summer 1948, Journal of Thames Barge Sailing Club (includes article on Everard). [SSBR]
13	'The Thames Sailing Barge may soon be a thing of the past', Thames Sailing Barge Preservation Society appeal brochure. [SSBR]

14	**14.a**	Thames Sailing Barge Match programme, 19.6.56. [SSBR]
	14.b	48th Medway Barge Sailing Match programme, 21.6.56. [SSBR]

15	F.T. Everard & Sons Ltd. - Pelham Jones 1937 - *Suavity* off Greenhithe, promotional print. [SSBR]

16	Trade union papers:

	16.a	Working Rules agreed between the Association of Master Lightermen and Barge Owners and the Watermen, Lightermen, Tugmen & Bargemen's Union, 2.5.1927, (Blue covered booklet (4" x 5½")).. [TUC]
	16.b	The Company of Watermen & Lightermen of the River Thames and The River Thames Watermen & Lightermen's Benevolent and Almshouse Benefit Fund, 34pps Annual Handbook, including tide tables for 1971 (3¼" x 5¼").. [TUC]
	16.c	Watermen, Lightermen, Tugmen & Bargemen's Union Contribution Cards, 1920, 1937/38, 1938, 1938/39, 1939/40, 1940/41, 1941, 1941/42, 1942, 1942/43, 1943, 1943/44, 1944, 1944/45, 1945, 1945/46, 1946, 1946/47, 1947, 1947/48.. [TUC]
	16.d	Terms of Decasualisation Agreement, 6.9.1967 (inserted in weekly pay rates) (4" x 5½").. [TUC]
	16.e	Watermen, Lightermen, Tugmen & Bargemen's Union, extract from transcript of evidence by Brother W. Lindley to Court of Inquiry, 20-21.10.1954.. [TUC]
	16.f	National Dock Labour Board, The Thamesman, Olympic Games, 1956 including Welfare in the Lighterage trade - message from W. Lindley - 12pps.. [TUC]
	16.g	The River Thames Watermen & Lightermen's Benevolent and Almshouse Benefit Fund, subscription deduction form (unsigned).. [TUC]
	16.h	White Paper, 1946 Ministry of Labour and National Service, Port Transport Industry, report of inquiry. . [TUC]
	16.i	The PLEBS, organ of the national Council of Labour Colleges, Vol. XXXVIII, No.11, November 1946.. [TUC]

17 Photographs:

17.a Two deck hands on coaster (2$^1/_4$" x 3$^1/_4$"). [NMM]

17.b Everard motor coaster dressed overall with pennant 'PRO....' (*Prowess*) (5$^1/_2$" x 8$^1/_2$"). [NMM]

17.c *Prowess* of London dressed overall alongside - postcard (found in Chief Officer's Log). [NMM]

17.d Sailing Barge *Cecil* of Rochester in the entrance to Hammersmith creek.

17.e Mounted 4 story terraced housing Riverside Gardens street party with Mayor. [H&F]

17.f Charrington, Gardner, Lockett lighterage roads (4$^1/_4$"x 3$^1/_4$").

Picture Sources

Where the word Photo appears, the name which follows is that of the photographer. The provider is identified, current source listed last. Sources are listed by page number and position.

OFC, top left: Photo, E.W. Carter, Lincolnshire County Council, Gainsborough Library, via Tony Farnham. **OFC, top right**: Fielder Archive, National Maritime Museum. **OFC, bottom**: Photo, A. Duncan, Ken Garrett collection. **10**: John Oxford Collection, Blue Circle Archive. **12**: John Baker collection. **13**: www.myhometown-oldphotos.co.uk. **15**: Photo, E.W. Carter, Lincolnshire County Council, Gainsborough Library, via Tony Farnham; **16**: Fielder family collection. **17**: The British Postal Museum and Archive, via Tony Farnham. **18, top**: Royal Navy Museum collection. **18, bottom**, Photo, R. Anderson, Ken Garrett collection. **19**: David Challis collection. **21**: Fielder Archive, National Maritime Museum. **22**: Fife County Libraries & Museums; Kirkcaldy Museum & Art Gallery. **23**: Susan Butler collection. **25**: Photo, A. Duncan, Ken Garrett collection. **26**: John Ritchie, Books Afloat, Weymouth collection. **28, top**: Photo, Nautical Photo Agency, Ken Garrett collection. **28, bottom**: Thurrock Museum collection. **29**: Ray & Barbara Woodmore collection. **30**: Photo, F.C. Gould, Tony Farnham collection. **31**: A.G. Linney collection, © Museum of London. **32**: London Borough of Hammersmith and Fulham. **33, top**: London Borough of Hammersmith and Fulham. **33, bottom**: London Borough of Hammersmith and Fulham. **35**: London Borough of Hammersmith and Fulham. **37**: Fielder Archive, National Maritime Museum. **38**: Ken Garrett collection. **40/41**: Mitchell Library, Glasgow City Archives. **42**: Fielder Archive, National Maritime Museum. **43**: Hugh Muir collection. **44**: Photo, E.W. Carter, Lincolnshire County Council, Gainsborough Library. **45**: Photo, A. Duncan, Ken Garrett collection. **46, top**: © English Heritage (Aerofilms collection). **46, bottom**: Thurrock Museum collection. **47**; © English Heritage (Aerofilms collection). **48**: Imray, Laurie, Norie & Wilson Ltd. **49**: London Borough of Hammersmith and Fulham. **51, top**: Sheila Hutchinson collection. **51, bottom**: Mike Sparkes, Norfolk Wherry Trust. **52**: Photo, Jack Harrison. **53**: Photo, A. Duncan, Ken Garrett collection. **54**: Beeld collection, Het Markiezenhof Historisch Centrum. **56**: W.S.P.L. Ken Garrett collection. **57**: © English Heritage (Aerofilms collection). **58**: Photo, E.W. Carter, Lincolnshire County Council, Gainsborough Library, **59**: Mersea Island Museum. **61, top**: Photo Wm. Lind, Ken Garrett collection. **61, bottom**: Photo, V. Allen, Ken Garrett collection. **62**: © English Heritage (Aerofilms collection). **63**:

B.O.C.M. Pauls Ltd., archives. **64**: Godfrey collection, Newham Heritage & Archives. **65, top**: Photo, P.T. Rayner, Ken Garrett collection. **65, bottom**: Photo, D, Brown, Ken Garrett collection. **66, top**: Postcard image, King's Lynn Forum. **66, bottom**: Postcard image, T.W. Acock, Wells-next-the-Sea. **67**: EWW, King's Lynn Forums. **68**: Richard Smith collection. **69**: Part of postcard image, Richard Walsh collection. **70**: Fotoalbum 506, Nedalco, Het Markiezenhof Historisch Centrum. **72**: Wayne Pritchett collection. **73, top**: S.S.B.R. Archive. **73, bottom**: © English Heritage (Aerofilms collection). **74, top**: Fotoalbum 506, Nedalco, Het Markiezenhof Historisch Centrum. **74, bottom**: W.S.P.L. Ken Garrett collection.**75**: Photo, P.A. Vicary, Fred Cooper collection, Ray Rush collection. **76**: Fred Cooper collection, Ray Rush collection. **77**: Fotoalbum 506, Nedalco, Het Markiezenhof Historisch Centrum. **78**: Fotoalbum 506, Nedalco, Het Markiezenhof Historisch Centrum. **79**: Beeld collection, Het Markiezenhof Historisch Centrum. **81**: David Challis collection. **82**: © Museum of London. **83**: General Register Office. **85, top**: Municipal Archive Zaanstad. **85, bottom**: Municipal Archive Zaanstad. **86**: © Museum of London. **89**: Photo, Grimsby Telegraph. **90**: John Baker collection, via Sheila Hutchinson. **91**: D. Brown, Ken Garrett collection. **92**: Photo, Tony Millatt, Mersea Island Museum. **94**: Municipal Archive Zaanstad. **95**: David Challis collection. **97**: Tony Allen collection. **98**: Robert Dennis collection. **99**: Doust & Co. archive, via Medway Archive and Local Studies Centre. **100**: Hull Daily Mail. **103, top**: Fielder family collection. **103, bottom**: Fielder family collection. **104**: London Borough of Hammersmith and Fulham. **106**: Photo, John Topham, Tony Farnham collection. **107**: Photo, Philip Kershaw, Fred Cooper collection, Ray Rush collection. **109**: Fred Cooper collection, Ray Rush collection. **110**: David Challis collection. **112, top**: Tyne Tugs website. **112, bottom**: Simon Bang collection. **115**: Poole Museum collection. **117**: British Sugar plc. archive. **118**: Fred Cooper collection, Ray Rush collection. **119**: Fred Cooper collection, Ray Rush collection. **120**: Punch magazine advertisement. **121, top**: Municipal Archive Zaanstad. **121, bottom**: Wilberforce House Museum, Hull Museums. **123**: Newbury Diesel Co. story website. **125**: Photo, Real Photographs Co. Ltd., Ken Garrett collection. **126**: Postcard, Richard Walsh collection. **128**: Photo, E. Taylor, Ken Garrett collection. **130**: © Museum of London. **131**: Fielder Archive, National Maritime Museum. **132**: Photo, Johannes Tjaden, Roger Wilmut collection. **133, top**: David Challis collection. **133, bottom**: Fielder Archive, National Maritime Museum. **135**: Fielder Archive, National Maritime Museum. **137**: Ray Perry collection. **138**: Fielder Archive, National Maritime Museum. **140**: Fielder Archive, National Maritime Museum. **141**: Allan C. Green collection. **142, top**: Postcard, Tony Farnham collection. **142, bottom**: Photoship.website. **143**: Fielder Archive, National Maritime Museum. **144**: Fielder Archive, National Maritime Museum. **145, top**: Fred Cooper collection, Ray Rush collection. **145. bottom**: Fielder family collection, via Tony Farnham. **147**: Bob Sheridan collection. **148**: Photo, Albert Herring, Fielder family collection. **149**: Photo, C.C. Beazley, S.S.B.R. Archive. **150, top**: David Challis collection. **150, bottom**: Photo David Hocquard, via Ken Garrett. **151**: Ken Garrett collection.

INDEX - GENERAL

Place names use the relevant historic counties. Page numbers in **bold** indicate illustrations.